UGLY DUCKLING PRESSE :: DOSSIER

Dear Angel of Death
Copyright © Simone White, 2018, 2019

Dossier Series
ISBN 978-1-937027-67-4
First Edition, First Printing, 2018
Second Printing, 750 copies, 2019

Ugly Duckling Presse
The Old American Can Factory
232 Third Street, #E-303
Brooklyn, NY 11215
www.uglyducklingpresse.org

Distributed by SPD/Small Press Distribution (USA), Inpress Books (UK),
Raincoast Books via Coach House Books (Canada)

Cover design and typesetting by goodutopian and Don't Look Now!
Set in Adobe Caslon with DTL Caspari titles
Printed and bound by McNaughton & Gunn
Covers printed offset by Prestige Printing and letterpressed at UDP
Cover paper is Mohawk Strathmore Premium Blazer Blue

This book was made possible, in part, by a grant from the National Endowment for the Arts, and by public funds from the New York City Department of Cultural Affairs in partnership with the City Council, and by the continued support of the New York State Council on the Arts.

Simone White

DEAR ANGEL OF DEATH

DOLLBABY

First, secure the milk
then quick I must show you
my body's inventing itself
that my body should make herself
ground for the great shock of suck
that, I
quaking metal in fixed
ground, I
site of infection,
I, arrowroot cookie
taste is the true prophetic word

Secure the milk
and I'll tell you
grammatical properties
of the pronoun
motherfucker

Secure the milk
and we'll talk about
"Marxism Leninism Mao-Tse Tung Thought"
which is milk thought
which is what I believe

4:18 am
left boob:
the baby
saw a spirit
clowning on the ceiling,
the thing or things not there,
certainly amusing.
the baby's face is kind of flat;
that's beatific. I scare easily.

Of the long poem I had said there could be
a secret text, a sacred accompanying text
unreadable but for its having been written
and erased. But how to establish secrecy?
Not undiscovered, nor buried, then unearthed.
Its paradigm is the burning bush; psychosis
matériel, madness of cause.
There must, I'm saying, be a listener, also mad,
ready with testimony to extinguish doubt.
There must be witness and whispering
and uncrated objects that have not been touched
except by these two.

The primary position taken by me as against
the secondary position (the backward, the prone);
that is the point. The point being
to run down the arbiters of licensing
with a demand for pictures. Show me
an image of your perfect listener.
Deep sound.
Trash musicality, folklore of the heard,
remnant of the flightlessly flapped wing,
I forbid. I forbid pathos.
And contrast. Forbid that, too.
Me in the primary position.

The primary position's rough justice being
to run down the arbiters of listening.
Put myself to the side of listening
Put myself over listening
Take a vacation from listening
and listening's homonym
udderance
and listening's key practice
"damnation."

On whose part comes such failure
of imagination? Upon whom does it come?
Upon nothing of threat.
Straddle this longing.
It is circular.
Its "self-regard,"
which is also flat,
abiding anti-calculation.

If we have failed to prosper,
or rather to become prosperous
in the sense that one earns silence
on the federal holiday of one's choice,
if we have failed in that,
in prospering according to proper functions
of the glands and of capital,
it is called poverty.
In the above example of hypotaxis,
weren't you her man?
Her man of opportunity.
So-called prospering.

Excellent French of the seminar,
many early years in language training,
of the language lab, of the contest.

Then French of the tutor. Bad French
Of the baby class, the first grade Mademoiselle.

French of one's own Fanon translation
Also the French of jealousy of tokenism,
The soft sexism of the academic job market.

What might be, yet never is because.
On Sunday one scrubs the toilet, in French.

French of the kitchen and of Colette,
of the nicest suitcase you've ever seen in Paris,
in her brightest trousers, drunk in Pigalle.

French of correct sense memory.
The sweet smell of familiar cock.
If you can still say that today in America,

cock. Familiar or favorite.
Do the French stand alone.

Perspicacious beyond health,
All things are effortless.
You milk the baby; it is effortless.
Your choices are beautiful.
You have read everything.
Let this be the reason
you go without
Deetjen's vacations.
Repetitive motions,
swept along by the overtures
of the injurious dance workshop.
This is no one's fault;
not my pussy's fault, nor yours.
It is deep February. You are not depressed.
Primary is new to you, primary red.
A soft and suckable red mushroom
reminds you of a nasty wen
or a witch bauble for striking
on black rocks.
Maybe the dancers will bust their wrists,
how careless and cheap
their twirling appears from this vantage.
White like the crystal Stacy has promised me
the mind grows light and visible ice.

You could get pink eye,
one would think,
putting your face on on the subway.
But, anything for Eileen.
An outline of face
preliminary to appearing at the sad gig
in the endangered garret.
Languor, like headrags, unfashionable.
At last, life is ordered the way you wanted
with once a week cleaning,
a child sleeping on his side (tiny man!),
chocolate cosmos renounced
As now,
in retrospect, the wicked nonce
happiness of cut flowers
all too plain,
solitude comes back on you.
Taking leave of the dynamism of organizations,
ad hominem attacks wash over you
from another dimension.
The mind wanders to Robert De Niro
at the club in Atlanta.
That would have been fun.
What do you know about capital really?
Perhaps the intelligence
characterized by willingness to stretch,
not proud of having learned the study habits
    of the white shoe,
is offended by burrowing actions.
Taking offense a lot, then.
The action of the day burrows.
The day is taken up in most bewildering
deflections of informational assault

by poet revolutionaries.
In English we don't say
I can't care about it.
I can't care, coming out the side of your mouth.
Where did you come by
your taste for blood.

SPRING POEM

Unless there was a turn in the way of things
all would continue to vibrate
with foreboding. Hazard littered
the pink tree bud.
Hazard would ruin the festival of the peony
if nothing was done, and soon.

An odour of scorched broccoli
followed you down
Fulton, then Clinton, then Second Avenue.
The olfactory sense pricked up
in concert with descent, its due
in the order of consciousness
coming round like psychosis
sooner or later.

Perhaps this person does not understand
the extent of my exuberance.
I was taking secret photos on the subway
that week of young black men
all in black and flowers;
trendspotting it was,
as well, an extended meditation
on the troubles
or where the testosterone package
has led. Francesca the bittersweet,

one expects to be visited in the nerves daily
by the tragedy of early middle age.
And yet. Who expects to break down

under the pressure. Not me. Ha.
Oh Lord. One resents His invocation
in the poems of others.

It was frustrating
my wish for a biscuit, a true biscuit
of White Lily flour
as I'm living now on cake
and meatballs.

FOR FLOSSIE

You won't remember the first time it was 1989 you were flanked by an Ankh and person I would learn to call your woman very soon and this would be things there would be a woman and I was something else other than early memory which is now perhaps memory of not having been noticed therapist would say of an invented hardship in long time of never mattering enough and seeking out long time of not mattering by finding in first moment definitive sensation of a given desire's co-existence within erasure. Possibly of a certain age body of a nineteen year-old wincing quality of woman who will never be presence of your body exactly in cinematic "past" the body which in 1989 began to be yours and became body of your woman became also body of the changing year I remember 2:17 am. Expectation is a curious thing to develop around the problem of not having been noticed or been absent or been without yet this was your hour to begin to expect you one or two minutes prior is expectation was. Once your woman within hearing you were gone teenaged gossips you know how you know the sex will be good or great or excellent none of these I remember what'd she know about it having any idea what good or great or excellent as at that time of being seventeen happily blundering into some truly excellent fucking arrogance and having at least sense to know 1990 it wouldn't happen unless you could relax a little about you know Kenneth Clark's bougainvillea trellis or fingerbanging whatsit out of doors I remember that. There was correspondence Bronx were there horses at that time or twenty years later riding lessons baseball hats I could be the kind of woman mothers love then now hard around the mouth set to trials over being without several places to live later a white cat and another woman same one you loved her deservingly what was I wearing skinnier so many boys I sort of loved at twenty-two when bourbon law review snuff bourbon and soda god a lot of bourbon where were you you called from maybe Ghana dunno next thing I knew you were in my bed so Ghana so few surprising number of nights this was never your way pancakes I imagine you were heartbroken which I was too stupid to know can't remember. More night visitation in Ft. Greene. Reluctantly one admits to having had a great deal of good or great or excellent sex but east coast apartments one is never *away* one is never one. One's mother is often correct. Several realms of protection averrals won't take I believe in the god of open mouths and the Sherwood Forest. I remember our only fight means nothing about money as to why to "make love" all night not sleep. Assuredly it was not possible not to persist hi Candace thanks to take advice at thirty after the breakdown although I had never felt better you don't stay. Several hotels. Once we fuck and I don't come. You are heartbroken and then you have a son and I was cooler than that I remember I know now it is possible to deny even how I have loved you and for how long for how very little indeed it costs except what is out of the flesh once is out forever and then we are forty and forty-two and forty-four and I have a son.

LOVE POEM

"you" tell me how fucked up you are
as if my secret were not general drift
in partial or limited attention on the spectrum
of whole attention or love
in the way "I" had hoped
this symptom or failure is ongoing
even now wounding myself
as another separation begins
turning back to keep a simple measure
to accurately say the cost
this kind of womanhood whose longing
is not to be made stupid in its face
as could be implied alors this woman
in her prom dress on the subway like that
like that lives for you in the measure
of stones' distance from the fully built

he grips my clavicle in the dead of night
with unexpected power
he moves the skin along the bone
under skin   cradle
this hard place
known to us in the dead night
of almost pain
I watch us work   to move away from each other
we grieve and press some virtual
line our muffled days

I write in secret to extend / the attention for channeling
going on without recourse / to interpretable phrases
games such as pinochle / are attention in retreat
secrecy shreds attention
makes for it unlikely perforations
so little gasps illustrate folding
one word over another / one is inside the other's attention
or conceptual field / you bring attention inside
in the way of by way of secreting / in a dump motel
where everyone would be looking
but for the proliferation of dumps /
your key witness

NICOLE EISENMAN, I NEED YOU TO MAKE A PICTURE

Nicole I saw you at the church and need your help. I think it's important to record relaxin's long term distortions. My legs are slightly bowed not from doing anything so that is immaterial. What about this gappy thing between my thighs there is something wrong with my hips they are stuck or something, I mean they get stuck when I move so there is an arc in trying to move forward so that every forward movement involves a circle that was not there before. When I bend over completely in Prasarita Padottanasana like my groin is released in such a way like I feel the turning of a ball of the joint in such a way that I imagine my hip joints as padded with cork there is a softness such as was not there a soft hole that was not there in the groin which is related to the gappy hips. My boobs are ruined and ought to be painted as soon as possible as I cannot say whether they are ugly or beautiful; they are a ruin so how do you show that or what do you do about change of that nature where overnight you were one thing and then unimaginable punishments and then you were out of that even if you are not religious or a very small child I think you need a picture showing this kind of bodily rage although I admire certain aspects or angles of what I now see as the brutal indent of a formerly powerful ass. And the way I am eating which cannot be pictured but might be symbolically "pictured" or I pick up and secretly eat carbohydrates I load in ways previously revolting to me as my fear of obesity is intense everlasting earned. I think my digestion is ugly. Returning to the privations of the past is tough despite years of trouble sacrifice of blood blisters under the toenails I sweated this muscle in the modern way with only moderate success. The limp is runner's knee.

TWO THINGS WERE HAPPENING AT ONCE

the ghoul bug's a practical terror
you cannot commune with
nor Klan idiot with a sickled knife
the rape sneak, however
I think I had medicalized a violence
I, too
slow to feel as usual
labor, then tear
where, "This mode of commemorating Christ
is not suitable to me,"
while sometimes I am like
your assessment of this thing's causation is faulty
in the following three ways
the rape sneak walking the earth   and the door of the house
blown open in explanation
for the baby, wind
inside, behind
a change in register announces itself
wishing at the wall of the Getty: cold white
I wished to be, to turn myself under your body
a globule in the mixing interest   of trollops and representatives
at Berkeley, I, too
cackling in the mirror

Then let this book be a glory hole I will lay on you the time my period returns and I spend all day shamed by thought that would not be jammed through anything. Fuck my thinking it is so undisciplined! I think and feel embarrassed and cannot stop sneaking around my imagination looking for ways to commit adultery in a thoroughly surveilled world or rather put myself in a psychological space where I would be myself again no one's wife and do what I want. Frankly I am jammed up even in fantasy which seems too effortful and for the birds in a 1970s sense of being for the birds all Mary Tyler Moore and the adults secretly tooting away at parties. Children of the age of AIDS, we learned. On the mercy of the book I place this accursed thing.

STINGRAY

Having had no proper family name I made do
with Stingray never loved a man so-called
for more than a generation black and white
suffer nameless conditions
instigated by the father's line of nobody
murmurs to the baby "goodnight nobody"
there is no longer any way to count
beneath the highways of the Eastern Seaboard
above the Mason Dixon line
underlie so many crossings

What to me the arched wing of a black Stingray
who think weeping over her vicious mouth
somnolent practice of stuck terror of the wave
is Stingray the atomic principle of giantism
make my whole mouth move around the fire
make the fire everywhere or cold
on this street Stingray where a man thinking his boat
beauty knowing moneys or leather, white leather
feeling however the killing power of the great sea monster
her haunch whip a think acquired as a gorgeous capital

Wait and sting why Odysseus
always in trouble with the one-eyed
what caused His love of lake demons
(her gauze whimple
under blacklit stars)
His very early anticipation
of the right guitar sound
its fullness, no
re-union of the ocean and the desert
just reflect on the history of the house

57 rays die in Chicago
for want of so lush a malapropism
I wait a long time outside the ocean
and your body sometimes nothing of images
dead brown and such like luminous captivity of the dead
repeated back to our obsessional contemporary
says back a weird lie
when inside me a bit of god comes out your mouth
as the command to feel you what
kind creature will you take me from being to what

Her mallow glamor warns
warmed in the glowering ripple light
this liquid this death to you
lady come under this death it is ablaze
in its blue white perfection hold your hand like a cup
water light will pour you into the whole day
the deafening memory of your tenth year
occurring in the space between sunup and sundown
on a plot the size of an hibiscus flower
you, miss

The Bicentennial was yesterday
write queer and muggy apparently evening
every minute the Declaration must be signed
firework on the barge child mind
to which no Superfund has yet gently repaired
get me a Stingray the color of slate
a little girl switchblade the horizon of which is an arc
gutter oil slick Delaware that horizon
is New Jersey a plot (her shore)
farms send blueberries and war

In this form it is impossible to be together
it is being nothing at all then cast in this court trick
vulvar form o clamped then
between together and nothing
forms of sand coarse pink edible
no seams along which to break
a black flag waves in hot wind
form of formless   a craft, a craft appears
materialized hot gas
raucous to suspend life outside of life

Shadows beyond wishing
and male news emplotted to hover
no wools or porcelain anywhere in sight
of the flat class
Stingray
vanities pool
heteronomous in the tight
grate
withdraw from earth
one fractal   initially

Retreat then
the slick thing quavered she said
of sediment rustling abashed
contemplation of stones rushing together
under the fresh
lake not the elementary bite of capital
give that is a wound
and she, raw, bloodless
could you bleed housed gowned
fucked in a prehistoric manner
still sea monster

The very source
or the veil
complete silence, the silent
inhalation or stopped time
time, being unmet
totally unregulated
slack and unreturned
threshing
the dna then
she becomes another one

DOG POEM

On this day 11 years ago my father died.
I watched him refuse death.
There was no reason to share this.
It was an indignity.
There is no refusing.
The brain stops even if until the last it performs miraculously the
    duty of remaining illuminated.
He died on an evening like this warm one in November.
Loose leaves blew around the parking lot as I drove away from the
    place of his death, a hospital.
I smoked with my mother's second sister just beyond the gate of
    the house my parents bought, owned and lived in together for
    twenty-six years.
I lived in that house, but did not live there then.
We smoked and a reporter came to the gate and asked her
    questions.
She was ashamed.
There was no need to answer her.
We did not answer.
We smoked.
The night was strangely warm, like so many peculiar Hallowe'ens,
    November in just a few days.
Autumn quiets or casts itself between the warm parts of air.
It fills spaces of warmth with cold.

On the eastern seaboard of the United States where now there is
    nothing like the four seasons we knew as children, I suppose
    I have come to understand ecological disaster in these limited
    terms, as fallen evening, as a reflection of a more general
    limitation of world ideas, inability to enter into discussions of

structure or apparatus without the help of lyric rendering.
It's not a matter of incomprehension—evening for death.
Vacant shacks on land the size of a town that once belonged only to my family deep in Scott County, Mississippi;
this for mine, or ours, and also, guns.
I first touched my grandfather's beloved hunting weapons at this "homestead."
Touching, an act that did not resemble in any way the late experience of inspecting, loading and discharging a 9-millimeter handgun.
Range shooting was an activity my father enjoyed, found amusing.
The unnatural power of tiny hand canons is disgusting.
When I found that my hands were neither large nor strong enough to manage an automatic weapon of this kind, for the first and only time in my life I shook all over, my arms and hands were shaking.
I could not participate further or again in this kind of family outing.
My family thought nothing of this.
There is one story about me as a melodramatic type—a swooner—which is utterly ridiculous.
Someone suggested a smaller gun, a .38-caliber revolver.
Apparently this was the gun for a woman prepared to manage the killing of a human person.

Now the local tragedy of my father's death passes.
It has passed through the writing of these sentences.
It is past.
The fleetness of death is most impressive, crushing in its casual completeness and simplicity.
The brain stops.
The heart stops.
Then there is no more breath, a sign that life has ended, its signal end, I suppose.

If, stay with me for a moment, I am not sure how to begin to
>   say this, it is the case that one takes the measure of vitality as
>   against the instantaneous cessation of all things, then to be alive
>   is to be held by or to hold the thread of being continuous.
One wishes on occasion for the relentless dailyness of living to,
>   what, go into retreat.
Retreat is a word I like.
For example, because you will not come to me, I decide I am going
>   to tell you something.
I decide that it will take a long time.
It will take as long as I want because you are not waiting, and I am
>   incapable of waiting.

Through the lens of another self I regard the actions of the mad
>   one.
I drop her anchor.
She is not physical.
We are together and apart, space, sparks, speed, as tonight the
>   sleepless baby shuddered in my arms, at last, at last away, we
>   wrest one another from the ordinary, rudely entwined at
>   deepest night.
Suddenly I see, not because of the dark, but in it, that this is a new
>   way to know the organization of time.
Leaning back with the child, limp in my arms, un-subject to the
>   sides of time, no longer given to a three dimensional vision
>   of time's progress as cubed units, which thing rises up as a
>   monstrous extrapolation from the illusion of lines,
I understand my baby, my mad self, as merely pricked by time's
>   stabbing proboscis.
Is the minor space of an hallucinated freedom nothing?
I'm asking what you think.

ENDINGS

… it concerns a tension that clasps together and transforms past and future … in an inseparable constellation. The messianic is not just one of two terms in [a] typological relation, it is the relation itself. This is the meaning of the Pauline expression 'for us, upon whom the ends of the ages are come face to face with each other.' … this face to face, this contraction, is messianic time and nothing else. … for Paul the messianic is not a third eon situated between two times; but rather, it is a caesura that divides the division between times and introduces a remnant, a zone of undecidability, in which the past is dislocated into the present and the present is extended into the past.

… insofar as messianic time aims toward the fulfillment of time … it effectuates a recapitulation, a kind of summation of all things, in heaven and on earth—of all that has transpired from creation to the messianic 'now,' meaning of the past as a whole. Messianic time is a summary recapitulation of the past…

The poem is … an organism or temporal machine, that, from the very start, strains toward its end. A kind of eschatology occurs within the poem itself. For the more or less brief time the poem lasts, it has a specific and unmistakable temporality, it has its own time.

— Georgio Agamben
*The Time That Remains:
A Commentary on the Letter to the Romans*

MOTHERHOOD IS A STATE OF HYPERVIGILANCE

Open arms gathering all so wide to hold everyone horizontally
growing, this way, flat in this way capturing each

pellet   stream

danger, failure to possess
holding what cannot be held
natural, weightless impact of pressure in tons

separate,   prostrate time
the weather of wails
appetites

a thin sliver of wax or wood between one time and another what is
    the impact
between one time and another more time and more succeeding
    separations
caroling he is coming

THE FIRST DAY

child, break the metal field of bared teeth
and cold seconds

all between
you, your grip of-difference, you are the lip of unknown

come through the end of no longer or not
child, unwill

                                          your eventful violence
is time myself

the dark wing flutter bare brush
        surgical knife over which your power to
                make everything a kind of cold meat
for your enjoyment

here to bear

all difference

the opening you make in time it is small
matter

he is the other world come through me

toward profuse starlings
most profound misreading of the words
splinter spectra
toward
he is unable to seize hold of himself as a whole
I am to serve toward and am toward

then

STATE

It is a fish It is a whale   the only food I have eaten

is from the floor as not from the floor

The wicked carport, it is hell, it is hopscotch

It is a gash It is forever falling on your right knee It is smooth It is

    white and glossy with pure bright blood

It shines on the lip of a milk-sated infant soft like a kitten

white kitten soft baby It is a fish It is a whale It is cold

It wants to be touched   like you It is soft you cannot imagine

Imagine I am saying   do it

Fish, whale, ship

Caducity, the falseness of TV, the food I could still eat in Casablanca

It is a truck, it is a grain

It is a fish, It is a whale, It is a garbage truck the only word I know

is *garbage*, ice cream, gorilla

You are, baby

the fish the whale the skylark

you you you you you you you you you you you you you you you

you

You have

It is

The naturalized beast

The scar

We are

It is

soft

do it   I am telling you

I announce

It is

WE ARE HERE TO SLOW TIME

[we are here to slow time to break over us not considering so much making poems but where poems come from

"Equilibrations"

create a space that escaped the grasp of power and its laws, without entering into conflict with them yet rendering them inoperative]

come, here, Angel
this is the center of time
time's backwater
her kerchief her bilge
come here
register
emergency

stand, here, Angel
her dust, her wind
of politics'
vented fire
ventricle left other
cracked
oar
we are in
that see

having been the arch mouth
having been the blank
through which the demon of circles
might
enter

what if
my own being
broken
is the new law

Angel, I am
dust
cover me
velvet   air
blue it is not light
is not invisibility
it is space
it is visit-
ation

How I have loved you and for how long. Promises afield. One gathers or arranges the scope of unkept promises, partly a function of memory, partly a function of organic remaining; I stay, therefore I remember what has not come to pass what drags, remains, is remaining. The field is a field of action and it is a field of smoke—to arrange is nothing, arranged nothing. Promises, radiant formations of intuited nothing; each a sluice, every other threatens to drown. Take the open space, the field. What has occurred also nothing, as between two others, incomparable between, event at all times. Perhaps there is another sun, for these gravities are evidence of unlikeness, distracting solutions presented by physical laws. From these, nothing cannot be derived, nor the field, nor promises, nor the coming flood of what can be called smoke, what is blown by the things not are not light between [us]. *Us* is a metaphor for nothing, for remaining in this nothing, which is a category of absolute destruction, absolute despair, absolute possibility. Take that space. Not position.

Hour in which I consider hydrangea, a salt or sand plant, varietal, the question of varietals, the diet of every mother I know, 5 pounds feels like 20, I have lost … I have lost, yes, a sense of my own possible beauty, grown external, I externalize beauty. Beauty occurs on the surface of plants; the sun darkens the skin of my child, he is so small, he is beautiful (I can see; it is obvious) and everything about him is beautiful. Because he is small, the bite of some insect —its venom—makes his hand swell. He appears to feel nothing. He smashes his skull against the floor. He screams. I hold him in my lap on the kitchen floor in front of an open freezer, pressing a pack of frozen clay against his forehead. He likes the cold. I see; it is so obvious. Hydrangea. When I move, when I walk pushing my child's stroller (it is both walking and pushing or hauling, sometimes, also, lifting; it is having another body, an adjunct body composed of errand and weight and tenderness and no small amount of power), I imagine I can feel this small amount of weight, this 5 pounds like 20, interfering with the twitch of every muscle in my body. As an object, a mother is confusing, a middle-aged mother with little spare flesh, I feel every inch of major muscle pulling against gravity and against the weight of my child, now sleeping. This is the hour for thinking hydrangea. Let no man look at me. I stop to brush the drowsy child's little eye. His face. He barely considers his mother. I am all around him. Why should he consider what is all around him? Perhaps what is missing is a subtle power of differentiation. I am in, therefore, a time of mass apprehensions.

The reeds shook. A wide flat ass cradled in leather pants. This man's body I know and this one; I know what happens in two years, in five in twenty. "Time passing." Strong here, weak here, breaks along the line of. Bowsprit/disaster. Moooooooring. Silent ululations of turtle-eaters, or turtles being eaten. Vagaries and unattended lists. Everywhere giggles or handstanding over the new death, inability to love, covered in sensation and distance, wrapped in the life happening, covered in it, like a cling wrap, of which there is none. Called for you yesterday and nothing happened. Happening, also an absurdity, poorly understood until guns appear. A duet of spun tops, a trio, a quartet. Add another instrument that can't be held with life of its own that trembles with its own interior g, world itself. Call it a ghost, call its music ghostly, call what I want to do with your body a silence, call it an aporia, call it exigency, call it leave-taking or rest, I don't care what you call it, call it having been created for the no place of taking hold inside the inside call heard in the reeds.

MESSENGER

> all things are recapitulated in him,
> things in heaven and things on earth
>
> — *Ephesians* 1:10

PREPARE no night creature accidental enemy
encounters return to us in witch cradles, monsters by a hairsbreadth
these our works melted no accident these fires these crashes
capitulate to what is meant by the past as a whole
melt, fall back into accomplishment the grasp of who
prepares to give the message

The SIDE is excruciating we find him there pained not knowing
and the curt blast come to him as aside, as from the original
side ripped from the first man eaten by the merciless Blank
I find your cries ridiculous
the SIDE is all magma it is where we are taken to get
what is coming

in the middle of our conversation the phone rang it was you from the other side I rang through it was you calling from the other side I staggered it was you laughing you were interrupting the progress of our conversation you were laughing there was thus no middle there was the connection which loomed in its oddness being duplicated in all the realities where it was taking place the laughter was warm it reminded me of body heat it was pure energy it was you from the other side ringing through it was you pressing your finger to the hollow of my throat

PROCESSING the summation of all things that transpire
all dust not equally black black rocks
DIAMONDS whirling afloat synthy-lag
not the organic wave
that is a thing to resemble absurdly taking the form of what it is
    not, for it is never the water
it is never the sound it is never the light

gruesome Nosferatu spreads its claw over the light, its spine curves
that wave, misshapen jealous curled Saturday
my synths, piteously, not yet messenger
these our works, "now" being merciless
being crushed as a matter of criticism into nonspecific talk
of waves, the little irresponsible pedals

those snares when trap music got hot
the illusion of bending the strings, or PROCESSING
at the site of the miraculous the idea was to rebuild that sound on
    the synths
to recapitulate the past happening inside the body of deliverance
pull the field into what's still what suffers FUTURE arrivals
This nowness I inhabit is a gift

I AM THE WOMAN OF YOUR FIRST MATURITY
it was a WOMAN it was a child with the sex of a man
she spoke the words of the dead, gusts, her black lips closed
he-I crouched:
we cannot write. your night messages fucked me up
you arrested discovery of any kind. your body's nearness interrupts
   all dreaming

the woman was LOUD, she was impossible to hear without opening
the possibility of hearing at the event of its first uncurling
in the clenched ear of a wet newborn, the form that
instructs us in hearing's plasticity, sculptural
ear of time, its, her, the WOMAN's voice
broke over the figure(s), she kept repeating I AM

I AM THE WOMAN
to the figures differentiating digitally in the dark of her making
at once PROJECTIONS of the arch-joke of human dwelling together
in this nothing and PROVOCATIONS, the messenger seethed,
ARTLESS
SERVANT of this place

ευαγγελος addresses the mother with no mate the mother who panics the mother who watches the others with dread and wonder the careless pleasure of other mothers in the presence of their children the hours spent in fear the isolation of motherhood the metempsychotic deprivation of sleep nothing you have is yours not even deposits of fat you are the nothing toward which the man nods in acknowledgment of your motherhood which is grand which is prostration which is the deactivation of all known powers which is the evacuation of power your share in the speechless condition of your baby speech rushes you freeze in the weakness of joint potentiality you cannot share yet you share you have no faith yet you must have faith this is a test this is not a test everything that was has been evacuated in your arms someone has fainted someone's got a mote in her eye someone is pricked by *ευαγγελος*, hunter

we cannot write if time stops
all the industrial deviltry
clockwork such as normal
proves nothing
BARBARIANS
curatorial possibilities involving depth involving
cutting tools the mighty,
magic, death's opposite these our losses
flashing intimately courtside
wealth and black excellence taking place
as a magnitude of economic pornography
ceaseless negro apocalypse
it never comes

yet the despicable enjoy a beautiful invisibility
what rains upon them, dollar bills, shit on tiny wings
her callipygian behind a new economic
edifice
secure in   secure in its statement of miniaturized
state logics

OPEN YOUR MOUTH
whose mother are you, get out of here
the men, the men cannot write
you are not a man
you have never been anything but
this image of the end not the end
there are no saints
there is between us
whisper, night, hunger, indeterminacy
monies
scratch it down I COMMAND you
be or come or don't

RESIST if you want
the absolute indeterminacy between inside and outside
LOATHING both earth and sky and everybody else
getting in on it
this is not your first time
said the WOMAN the light

tread of masculine youth, glide upon his skateboard
a complex organization
threatening to lift itself so, outside physics
dismount the thing
wielding it in one hand like a weapon
everybody get in on it

no, just me, it's me who wants in on it

not the first time between your selves, down there
imagine, next,
alongside his joy
[how to listen to the body of a black man
in flight] he is always
about to knock somebody out

the joy between yourselves [flight, Michael, several decades,
converge with the value of having no body fat]
I, too, have wanted this power
said, the WOMAN,
I, too, invent the mercies of being within and without
the Mahgreb, the Carolinas and the West Coast

PROCESSING, our works
being births
inseparable from
desire
for him
love has no reason

she, I, now
was on her back, she was counting
a penetrating numerical hum through her
all these churches, sacred music
was the condition of possibility for sacred music
imagine what was now possible

this with a half-smile, the half-smile of a woman
who commands the silent rock

DEAR ANGEL OF DEATH

was there no way to be genuinely broken…was there no way to be genuinely whole

— Nathaniel Mackey
"Djbot Baghostus's Run"
From a Broken Bottle Traces of Perfume Still Emanate

I don't give two splats of an old negro junkie's vomit for your politico-philosophical treatises, kiddies. I like noise. I like big-ass vicious noise that makes my head spin. I wanna feel it whipping through me like a fucking jolt. We're so dilapidated and crushed by our pathetic existence we need it like a fix.

— Steve Albini

The question remains: whether and how to mark (visually, spatially, in the absence of sound, the sound in my head) digression, citation, extension, improvisation in the kind of writing that has no name other than "literary criticism."

— Fred Moten
In the Break: The Aesthetics of the Black Radical Tradition

Quo Vadis?

We are casting around somewhat desperately for an approximation of the human qualities which, for us, form the basis of true connection or near miss. We are cast about or away and must use a sense of qualities as belonging to ourselves and others to make an assay.

To have already rejected the qualities of being Mickey Mouse—feeling surpassing the armaments of liquid masculinity—and never to have had the products with which to build. Black radio leaps by decade when we go to it in terms of memory. We make culture this way, entirely in retrospect. What must be delineated is primary revulsion; to see outside the apparently open book and at the same time to read it: "As for reminiscing, this is a phenomenon more strongly marked by activity than reminding; it consists in making the past live again by evoking it together with others, each helping the other to remember shared events or knowledge, the memories of one person serving as a reminder for the memories of another"

In reverse of rejection revulsion reversion retrospection redrawing review remind recognize reminisce remembrance recollection

stubbornly persistent contextual negativity beginning knowledge of consistently pleasing immemorial connection

staging or reconstructing the human qualities which, for us, form the basis of what has been considered the same as

"it is super R&B and you won't like it because it is too slow and a tad boring."

Because it is too slow, you won't like it, and boring. You won't like a very abbreviated list informed by a book I've been reading on the way sounds come to stand for existence, for the commonly drawn marks that show togetherness as if we are—because we are—still required to make marks that remind us of the basic animal nature of our complex form of life.

As: up a cave without a piece of fucking charcoal.

An abbreviated list to make soft, to undo the R&B of my mind today. A set that sets a soft disgust. Steering clear and what's not to like in open access (to what has yet to be established as a philosophy of sortie). R&B establishes a spread for affective recon, where everybody is pressed together and recovering from pressing, as if that is the world.

Smokey Robinson, Tears of a Clown
James Brown, Get Up Offa That Thing
The Time, 777-9311
Prince, Adore, If I was Your Girlfriend, Darling Nikki, Bambi, I
    Wanna Be Your Lover, When You Were Mine, Do Me Baby,
    Anna Stesia, Ballad of Dorothy Parker
Rufus/Chaka Khan, I know you, I live you, Sweet Thing
R Kelly, More and More
Aaliyah, Rock the Boat, One in a Million, Come Over, Are You
    That Somebody?
Isley Brothers, For the Love of You, Groove with you, Footsteps in
    the Dark, Voyage to Atlantis, Brown Eyed Girl, Summer Breeze
Rick James, Dance With Me
Teena Marie, Square Biz
Mary Jane Girls, Candy Man
Cameo, Candy
Zapp, Computer Love, Dance Floor
Patti Labelle, If Only You Knew
Luther Vandross, A House is Not A Home, Never Too Much
Madonna, Lucky Star

Kleer, Intimate Connection
Al Green, Simply Beautiful
Bobby Caldwell, Open Your Eyes
Bobby Womack, You're Welcome
Womack & Womack, Baby I'm Scared of You
Guy, I Like
702, Steelo
Total, Sitting Home
Carl Thomas, I Wish
Rell, Love For Free
LaToiya Williams, Fallen Star
Mariah Carey, Breakdown
Hall & Oates, Can't Go For That
Ike &Tina, Proud Mary
Phyllis Hyman, Living All Alone
Terrence Trent D'Arby, Wishing Well
Harold Melvin & The Blue Notes, *Wake up Everybody*
Teddy Pendergrass, I Don't Love You Anymore, Turn off the Lights, Love T.K.O., The More I Get, The More I Want
Donny Hathaway, A Song for You
Spank Rock & Big Freedia, Nasty
Marvin Gaye, *Here, My Dear*, *What's Going On*, Inner City Blues
Roberta Flack, *First Take*
Howlin' Wolf, Smokestack Lightening
Jimi Hendrix, Killing Floor
Al Green, Simply Beautiful
Parliament, *One Nation Under a Groove*
Grace Jones, Pull Up to the Bumper, Nightclubbing, Walking In the Rain, My Jamaican Guy, La Vie en Rose
Nina Simone, House of the Rising Sun
Rose Royce, I'm Wishing on a Star
Richie Havens, Freedom
TV on the Radio, You

The Chambers Brothers, Time Has Come Today
Ann Peebles, I Can't Stand the Rain
Isaac Hayes, Hyperbolicsyllabicsesquedalymystic
Curtis Mayfield, *Superfly*
Deniece Williams, Silly
Joan Armatrading, *Joan Armatrading*
Minnie Ripperton, *Perfect Angel*, *Adventures in Paradise*
The Spinners, I'll Be Around
Fishbone, *Truth & Soul*
Cody Chestnut, Bitch, I'm Broke
Trey Songz, Put My # in Yr Phone
The Temptations, Just My Imagination
Erykah Badu, *Baduizm*
Sam Cooke, Cupid
Estelle, Shine
Otis Redding, Mr. Pitiful, Sitting on the Dock of the Bay
Aretha Franklin, I Never Loved a Man
John Legend, Ordinary People

It is super R&B and you won't like it because it is too slow and a tad boring.

What is black boredom? Out of curiosity, granting the possibility of the neurotic, the slow, unwieldy and short; the being of black rejection or seeking outside the previously elaborated book of making as black; the slipshod and inelegant black, the tuneless and impotent, the smeared boot-black pooling at our pretty neck.

Ne te quaesiveris extra.

Music is a huge therapeutic vehicle for me.... Spiritually metabolizing these things, I've come to realize that I need to practice openness like it's a sport. I think it would be such a shame to feel life as a burden the only time I get to live it. For me, the openness of my live show is a symbol of and a really important site of my work to fight negativity and depression and self-enclosedness, and really fight for intimacy and community.

— Tom Krell

R&B feeling's doubling proposing (I am open I am open to you I am available I am available to you my body is yours I am available to be stolen) is characteristic slippage between human qualities as America. Characteristic slippage on memory and marks, as simultaneously an act of gauging and erotic softness or exchange and of being inside the felt pleasures of others. You don't like it; it's not for you; yet nothing is wrong with it—R. Kelly peeing on people. No one objects to taking up the desire of one who always feels like making love: that is only making more and more blackness to sing, to shuffle and break down.

Contradict: to establish some primary hatreds, head off the radicalization of black feeling by way of black music; by way, in particular, of perceived dramatic changes in the present time's attitude toward it. To contradict, then, the absolute status of what black music is presumed to come from, to describe what cannot presently be described by going with the feeling of unwanted feeling, feeling boredom, feeling mistake, feeling mis- or manhandling, feeling isolation, feeling revolt, feeling targeted, feeling serious attraction to the claim of some unreconstructed bigot (notwithstanding the jolt he himself pulses through "My Black Ass," doubling proposing) that we have been weirdly loving toward "two splats of an old negro junkie's vomit," feeling (flowering, ambivalent) that this love can come to an end, that it might be over.

※

Throw on another goddamned Phoenician!

I cannot get off the first page of Amiri Baraka's *Digging*. Like his "Dark Lady of the Sonnets," this small text exemplifies the intensity of Baraka's prose exertions over the philosophy of feeling black through the related experiences of playing and hearing (calling out through and being called to respond through) music, the poetics of which has dominated for quite some time (since it happened) the space we speak of when we speak of "the Music" today. To trouble any aspect of feeling black, in part because of the Music, I need to deal with this page as an image—graph or map, notations indicating the terrain or shape—of the territory.

Look at this page:

Introduction

A great song arose, the loveliest thing born this side of the seas. It was a new song. It did not come from Africa, though the dark throb and beat of that Ancient of Days was in it and through it. It did not come from white America—never from so pale and hard and thin a thing, however deep these vulgar and surrounding tones had driven. Not the Indies nor the hot South, the cold East or heavy West made this music. It was a new song and its deep and plaintive beauty, its great cadences and wild appeal wailed, throbbed and thundered on the world's ear with a message seldom voiced by man. It swelled and blossomed like incense, improvised and born anew out of an age long past, and weaving into its texture the old and new melodies in word and in thought.
W.E.B. DuBois

One of the most beautiful explications, as analysis and history, of "the Music" comes from Du Bois, in his grandest work, *Black Recontruction in America*. So, because the good Dr. combines the material social world with and as the origins of Art. The Earth & the Sky.

So *Digging* means to present, perhaps arbitrarily, varied paradigms of this essentially Afro-American art. The common predicate, myself, the Digger. One who gets down, with the down, always looking above to see what is going out, and so check *Digitaria,* as the Dogon say, necessary if you are to dig the fartherest Star, *Serious*.

So this book is a microscope, a telescope, and being Black, a periscope. All to dig what is deeply serious. From a variety of places, reviews, liner notes, live checking, merely reflecting, the intention is to provide some theoretical and observed practice of the historical essence of what is clearly American Classical Music, no matter the various names it, and we, have been called.

The sun is what keeps this planet alive, including the Music, like we say, the Soul of which is Black.

In order to look at the page, before we begin to read the words, professionally or unprofessionally, of, first, W.E.B. Du Bois, then Baraka, what actions must we take or must we take part in? I mean this both somatically and in terms of thinking. What takes place when I do what I am invited to do by virtue of Baraka's assertion that Du Bois' image (all that he is) and some of his language must appear before us as a matter of establishing a point of origin and a standard of excellence? Before I read, I see a block of text, and the name, "W.E.B. Du Bois," which functions as a picture and a mode of transport toward a variety of ideas relating to the intellectual significance of black persons in the history of the idea of America. The picture that is made by setting the texts together, as Baraka has done here (as, I will show, Nathaniel Mackey does, as Fred Moten often does) proposes the long quotation as a visual/verbal bridge that shatters the isolation between the thinking and writing that is in front of us—before us—on the page *and* writing that is before us, figuratively, as the sum of what is in our minds now under the sign of reading *and* writing that has come before us in time. This is a manner/matter of composition and citation. We are moved, physically, by this manner of over-writing to place ourselves as readers, eye to eye with "the previous." Giorgio Agamben writes of the "strategic function" of disguised or hidden citations in Walter Benjamin's work:

> Just as through citation a secret meeting takes place between past generations and ours, so too between the writing of the past and the present a similar kind of meeting transpires; citations function as go-betweens in this encounter. ... This work consists not so much in conserving but in destroying something. In [Benjamin's] essay on Kraus we read, "[Citation] summons the word by its name, wrenches it destructively from its context, but precisely thereby calls it back to its origin; at the same time it 'saves and punishes'."

I acknowledge a similar order of linguistic intimacy, similar insofar as the characteristics of intertextuality remain human across time and facilitate our communications with all who have written before us, including the dead, and in that the intertextual is, as well, orthographically/aesthetically hybrid, so that words themselves speak of and to each other and become formation(s) and achievement independent of their agentic inscription. But I'm concerned with an historical order of aesthetic desire where, so unlike what Benjamin and Agamben describe, citation makes a visual/verbal bridge that implies a wish to lay or throw down with "the previous" by virtue of being fully given over to and in its presence, capitulating and racapitulating. The ocular and intellectual stress induced by attempting to read more than one text at a time—thick citation, big block, frequent repetition of the name of one's antecedent-interlocutors, archival or on-the-scene—intensifies textual interplay. Reader and text (must/do) draw close. I'm saying the order that constitutes the history of ideas as murmurings between Du Bois and Baraka, the masculine order of black writing, is an order that values being seen together: it is an order of claiming being together, not of hiding, not of disguise, not of suppression. The compositional assertion that the texts must be read together means something.

In *Nature*

> ...wise men pierce this rotten diction and fasten words again to visible things; so that picturesque language is at once a commanding certificate that he who employs it, is a man in alliance with truth and God. The moment our discourse rises above the ground line of familiar facts, and is inflamed with passion or exalted by thought, it clothes itself in images. A man conversing in earnest, if he watch his intellectual processes, will find that a material image, more or less luminous, arises in his mind, contemporaneous with every thought, which furnishes the vestment of the thought. Hence, good writing and brilliant discourse are perpetual allegories. This

imagery is spontaneous. It is the blending of experience with the present action of the mind. It is proper creation. It is the working of the Original Cause through the instruments he has already made.

Let's, therefore, take Baraka's construction of the first page of *Digging* as an incantatory act of textual image-making and declaration of alliance with [black] "Soul"—a remainder in persons of the Original Cause—that is also a rejection of a certain scholarly, and also philosophical, understanding of originality in general, even or especially philosophical understanding as it is pushed into a spiritual place via Agamben and Benjamin. Baraka, therefore, invites us to re-think certain questions of (black aesthetic) history as that which systematically explains the black original. That which is original is spiritually marked in the ways that Hortense Spillers has theorized, and also orthographically marked: these marks-become-writing fasten the original to the past and herald the possibility of, not separation from the antecedent, but mutual release from the antecedent's conditions of impossibility.

※

"One of the most beautiful explications, as analysis and history of 'the Music' comes from Du Bois, in his grandest work, *Black Reconstruction in America*. So, because the good Dr. combines the material social world with and as the origins of Art. The Earth & Sky."

The legal doctrine (also fiction) of *relation back* comes to mind when I try to unfold the way Baraka touches Du Bois by way of *Black Reconstruction*. Relation back establishes a structure that moves events that occur in the present, but ought to have occurred in the past, backward in time in order to meet the requirement that the event exist as cognizable at all, in the Court's view. This doctrine does not alter space-time, but it takes time under the wing of the law in an unfriendly way in order to rout its effects; to choke it out. If you re-turn to the passage Baraka wants you to relate to as a way of remembering the imaginary provenance of the explication of the rising "great song" —in a chapter hilariously titled "The Coming of the Lord: How the Negro became free because the North could not win the Civil War if he remained in slavery. And how arms in his hands, and the prospect of arms in a million more black hands, brought peace and emancipation to America"—you will find Du Bois in the grip of this odd text's haunted visitation of Emancipation as an incomplete, ever-dividing, receding-as-it-arrives, historical nonevent. (I have written, in *Unrest*, about at-least-doubled ways of hearing the honorific "Dr.") Reconstruction: an epistemological disaster of proportions so great that writing its history necessarily throws down the gauntlet of *telling history as the act of disabuse*; telling the history of Reconstruction is the act of becoming disabused of some bullshit. The text *Black Reconstruction in America* is a major work insofar as it embodies or enacts the practice of poetically placing the mind elsewhere, *backward* in the direction of freedom, in the critical position of review, moving to the example of Reconstruction from the perspective of the black as a "case" of critical desire to re-order space-time in the interest of the future. Or, as Du Bois puts what he says up-front—"three movements, *partly simultaneous and partly successive*...the swarming of the slaves to meet the approaching Union armies;...slaves [being] transformed in part from laborers to soldiers fighting for their freedom...organization of free labor after the war" —somewhat later, an account of how the "black folks' Apocalypse" had a chorus of "free, free, free." Three times, moving.

Baraka demands relation back to the critical activity of explicating the freedom song and not the song, the grandness of the work *Black Reconstruction in America* and not the "great song," "because" (this is Baraka positing predication or cause, not me) what is made grand comes that way as a result of Du Bois' recognition of the fact that it is impossible to detach the problem of the origin and existence of (the art of) the Music from the problem of "How the negro became free" etc. The great song will repeatedly be "new" insofar as the Lord keeps coming and blacks are repeatedly taken up into the historical convulsions or pulsations resulting from the first, *grandest*, emancipation.

Note that the sung song itself is *imagined as heard by Du Bois*, then *imagined by Baraka as an explication of the heard*, the song never actually having been in the presence of either of these two. Whatever is great, lovely, and new about "it" is some third-hand information, some already ready-to-be-explained information. Not from Africa, not from America, not East, not West, "seldom heard by man." Du Bois' turns of phrase occupy negative rhetorical space—not this, not that, "tones" nonetheless (humanly) heard, its "incense" drawn in, its "weave" sensed *intelligibly*, phonemenologically, by *the world*—anticipating the groundwork of making the whole world Africa by way of explosive invention and dissemination of invention (of something from nothing) by way of the Music. One explosion re-compacts the dust stirred up by the unprecedented movement around the earth of bodies that initially cause the appearance of the New World Black, constituting a real physical redistribution of black presence about the world. Another explosion *will be the explication of the heard*, the "old and new melodies of word and thought" that Du Bois signals the presence of, the arrival of, in *Black Reconstruction*.

Baraka relates back to Du Bois who "combines the material social world with and as the origins of Art. The Earth & Sky." It's important to listen closely to that. Where the origins of art are the middle term or *tertium quid* that is the black personal between "material social conditions and (period) The Earth & Sky," without a known grammatical procedure that describes relations proper to this new wild combination.

Baraka's whole proposal of *"Digging"* "meaning" (intending and signifying) "to present" not only the thing/object but also oneself as "One who gets down, with the down, always looking above to see what is going out, and so check Digitaria, as the Dogon say, necessary if you are to dig the farthest Star, Serious" is deeply disturbing. I am stuck on why I cannot quite perceive in the discourse of digging those actions done to the thing that has been gotten down on or gotten with, looked up and down. Ask a woman what happens when a thing is acted upon in any of these gendered ways. (I want to get with her. I got with her. She could get it.) The more-than-whisper of sexual domination in the coverage of the verb "to dig"—domination that need not be gendered male, but tends to come that way in the sense that Bob Marley means when he says that God "come black"—seems to me to conflate the existence of the personal "out and gone" with some variation of being in a top position.

In other words, I do not hear Baraka speaking here of the necessity of going down in order to get down, which is not the same as "getting with the down." When I am "with" the down, I am always free to get up and leave, to go back to the highly preferable up. Baraka prefers the up and out. Up and out implies the whole universe of digging.

I'm suggesting that the action of relating back, Baraka to Du Bois, and forward in time with the infinitely off-put coming of freedom is *infinitely* complex and that this complex action puts the balance of "down," "up," and "out" into crisis such that digging (and all that is implied by what is now a traditional method of interacting with the explosive inventions that have no name other than black music) starts to look like a lame description of the practice of the art, the theory of the practice of the art, and the theory of its appreciation. Without doubt, I'm moved by the elements of reverence for and desire to come into a far-out contact with actual works and the intellection of their coming to pass that Baraka describes. I'm still suspicious of Baraka's all-too-human inability to perceive the ways in which "digging" valorizes and throws shade over his stylized manner of turning toward and incorporating Du Bois' meditations; almost as if the style, the manner of designating the descent, were more significant than its nature, more important than describing the (fascinating) mechanics of the (fascinating) achievement—these are poetics —of the *tertium quid* that "was and is" black art that embodies the space-time chorus that is "free, free, free."

What is to be made of the hypothesis that Baraka wishes to fold into Du Bois, to fit *la Baraka* into a space of the past that Du Bois was once, in *Black Reconstruction,* able to unlock and to occupy by "merely reflecting" (Merely reflecting! So empty, even of the voices of the dead, was the space of writing on the historical problematic of "free"!)? That, now dead, Du Bois partially fills up and haunts explanation of the poetry of the poetry of freedom; that Baraka, now dead, desired [t]his space. That the double metaphor that is the Music and its black soul (their proposals of transcendence/ purity working at cross purposes) is nothing less than and nothing more than movement in the direction of theorizing an embrace inside the physical space the phoneme occupies between thought and language, between thought and its expression. That this purring originates nowhere and registers nowhere on the scale of human vibrations (air and flesh, all our vibrations); it doesn't sound like anything. That the practice of black aesthetics or black aesthetic theory, as Baraka says, "theoretical and observed practice of the historical essence of what is clearly American Classical Music," is not simply to tell the socio-cultural history of the Music as a vehicle for black culture and thus to tell the story of a people, as Baraka used to put it, nor to tell the story of possible enjoyment of black life through deep and accurate transcription of structures of feeling. That what is at stake in music-centered theories of black art/making black art is indeed "a new kind of morality"—a communal/cultural practice in itself, for itself; these men giving language to each other as its own kind of wanting to be together and wanting to be loved; a kind of freedom, which they see represented in the togetherness fabled in the calling and the responding and improvising and masking Baraka described once (yet, "Nothing was more perfect than what she was," where Holiday's perfection-in-death is severed by Baraka's subtle, if lush, grammatical operation from the live, experienced togetherness in the club, in the interview, in the Cedar Bar, in the letters): music as "instructive way beyond the confines of the venues in which it takes place and the particular musical culture in which it takes place, way beyond music itself."

I'm assuming that Baraka and his thought, especially his writing about the metaphysical and liberatory function of black music as a thought-case, have been folded into a black interior (a place I am suspicious of, though I think it exists) where he has been joined by those, like me, seeking to look out via the black person's periscope of which he speaks on that first page of *Digging*. I'm noting that a space of black American thought that was once officially empty— but not really, though—has become quite full. Membership in this club of undesirables who theorize the undesirable is policed and fought over just like everything else. I want to build a structure for exploring the mechanism of this black intellectual infolding, a word that became part of my vocabulary and this experiment via the work of Susan Howe, except I recall that Moten brought it in already via his reflections on the "spatial politics of the avant-garde." I'm going to argue that the interventions of Nathaniel Mackey and Fred Moten from the 1980s up to and including today, appropriately for the present times of both, take off from the language Baraka leaves in the space he folds into with Du Bois. Baraka's transcriptions of feeling, his witness to feeling in and through his listening to music, fill up a whole other related area of the universe of digging to involve the Music only secondarily and *certainly* metaphorically, beyond the question of whether the Music bears a black soul or the existence of the black soul, period. Continuous arousal of the question of the mechanics of the fold, the question of the manner in which relation back to other thinkers is practiced and acted upon by any artist or critic who celebrates and consecrates *Baraka's* relationship to the said, is in a complicated dance with the notion that real black expression tends to the unspeakable. Digging Baraka is digging the Black Art of Black Music is belief that black soul is movement outside the word of white supremacy's denial of black existence, which contains the possibility of spontaneous pleasure, which is beauty. Digging is a theory of the time-space boundary of black thought that hypothesizes a way to get to the outside of white totality, of white supremacy's word, which always, always, refuses the capacity of black people to move in a motivated way together through time-space, toward the end of white supremacy, which is freedom, or also, the end of time.

Reach for the "fartherest Star" is intellectual gesturing toward a furiously local rupture inside thinking formations that are still being built by individuals whose relations to one another are subject to dispute at the fundamental level of whether or not these individuals are capable in the first place of making a thought tradition in relation solely to one another, and the associated terror & refusal of terror by the individual constituted as without ties about the nature of ties. The rupture is caused by disagreement about what must be held in a state of arrest by thinking and what can be transcribed as unthought, where the extraordinary comes about by trying to get in a different place in relation to thinking about previously Serious or cosmic historiographies of rupture—how to get away.

This is about how to learn. This is about a tradition of being interested in "the aesthetic genealogy" of what takes place via the performance of black music by black persons and by persons who are not black (*including* consumption of these performances) who know themselves to be, aspirationally, taking part in radical desire to test new arrangements of the self, desire that has been called a "freedom drive," "this special ontic-ontological fugitivity of/in the slave."

Here are some passages from Moten's *In the Break* that, as of this writing, take up a lot of the air of the Serious in terms of a genealogy of this tradition, for which I have not yet been willing to provide a definition. (Moten offers "asymptotic, syncopated nonconvergence(s)" of "event, text and tradition," "Africa, Europe, and America," "outness, labor and sentiment" by way of periodization, geography, and blackness):

> I have been preparing myself to hear what is transmitted on frequencies outside and beneath the range of reading. Notes composed in the interest of that preparation: phrases: [29]

> Charles Lloyd, asked to comment on a piece of his music by a radio interviewer, answered, "Words don't go there."

> n 29. In the absence of reading, either or both of these terms [notes and phrases] might be just as reducible as wsord or sentence. Part of what I'd like to relate is the way *Taylor's (work art ritual performance music poetry)*, the way that which is of Taylor, renders all of these terms unavailable. Nevertheless I must retain them, at least for a minute, otherwise I Can't Get Started.

Don't we have to be interested in the oscillations of space and time enacted in the theatricality of criticism's *nothing gesture*, the gesture of making notes on what we have read and heard when it makes way for an otherwise impossible togetherness (of Moten, Lloyd, Taylor, then by way of Gershwin, untold plays upon the initiating standard combination)? *To fold, then to crumple, to smudge, to consign to the dustbin.* Moten is prepared—in the footnotes—to refrain from naming form, dealing instead with the way in which the black folks' Apocalypse is an event that might be *anything*, something in between preparatory and performed sounds and words. The question becomes how we will act or react when we find ourselves no longer able to hold steady in the nothing gesture: when the reticent beauty of being prepared to suspend the terms of reading and writing give way to notational and epistemological pressures, so that Baraka's work in the early sixties is not just

> situated as the opening of [that ontological field wherein black radicalism is set to work], as part of a critique immanent to the black radical tradition that constitutes its radicalism as a cutting and abundant refusal of closure. Or Baraka's lingering in the broken rhythms of the field where blackness and black radicalism are given in and as black (musical) performance, in and as the improvisation of ensemble, amounts to a massive intervention in and contribution to the prophetic description ... of communism that is, as Cedric Robinson has written, the essence of black radicalism.

So Baraka's work becomes the *sine qua non* of critical dependence upon notions of the immanence of improvisation, the immanence of ensemble, the immanence of certain sexualized "communism" to the free being of the black as maker of her own ways and works.

What happens when the improvisation of Enlightenment or modernism or (the philosophy of) (the end of) philosophy—as predicated on the eradication of a certain obsession with differentiated, representative, and representational identity—is lost? What chance does music, the music of the poem, the music that prompts the poem, the music that is prompted by the poem, give us to arrive at such an improvisation? How is such an improvisation to be recalled if its source grows more and more remote, separated from us by the death, by the distance of Miles?

I do not wish to be dragged into the thicket or walk along the ridge of a previously described genealogy, even when what has been described is nuanced almost to the point of "critical despair," acknowledged as "always on the verge of lyrical scandal," the scandal of having misunderstood the constitutive boundaries of our difference and our love, even while we did not know that we misunderstood and went on blamelessly, without error.

I was trying to get *off* this page.

☼

the letters respond to the music's ongoing call

— Nathaniel Mackey
From a Broken Bottle Traces of Perfume Still Emanate

Nathaniel Mackey, writing on the work of Wilson Harris, describes a "mixed, middle ground that privileges betweenness" as the "realm" to which art belongs and aspires. (Let's allow that echo with Baraka's formulation of black art as *tertium quid* between the material social and Earth/Sky.) For Mackey (a Florida/California black), Harris (a Guyanese black), as opposed to Du Bois (a Massachusetts haint), represents the scale of *grand* authorship in the epistemological territory that matters: the territory is diasporic and takes the cross-cultural for granted. And that taking for granted is symptomatic of—even as it constitutes—a major shift in the territory upon which (black) art is given: we are between earth and sky and also "between" the World and Africa. What becomes of the spiritual duality of the black confined to America in the aesthetic sense elaborated by Du Bois (we could also look at this through the eyes/essays of Ralph Ellison) through Baraka?

A few further words on the stakes before I try to describe the shape that Mackey's surveille imposes on a map of this epistemological territory, a shape that is not exactly, not quite, continuous with or incorporated by the historical formation that I am trying to show as an origami thing, or napkin, upon which the map is drawn, and then folded/unfolded/re-folded. (Not to mention the tangent formed by Paul Gilroy's reach for "the Music," belonging also to the original if insufficiently crystalline "triangle" whose center is the Caribbean Sea; not to mention *Hambone*, Mackey's curation of the space within or upon which a map *could* be drawn: an uncharting.) Stakes have to be thought in relation to both a *cartography* and a *discourse*: what are the discursive materials that make notions of chartability/axis/point/ edge, and therefore, fold, relevant in the first place?; what is required if the expression of Du Bois, Baraka, Mackey, Harris, Moten is to be understood as an order and how does this expression call for order to begin to take place or begin again? Relevant to what? What does it mean to enter a league of discussion where innovation, persistent beginning again, is impossible to dislodge, like a pit in the throat of statements regarding the nature of tradition; where t*he notion that invention is radical in itself* is held so close, gatherings of momentum that come off the one could be considered indecent (or, maybe, (purposefully) impossible to detect, if you look very close, or, if you fail to look very close)? Once I get it in my head to get up out of a place, then what happens, if the kind of straight movement that typifies the line is formally and theoretically forbidden me? *How's the map happen?* What is a map of the instinct to get up out? What do I get out of author/ship?

Where there is the notion that invention is radical in itself, there is nothing to trace but for "insistence that constant artistic innovation is at the heart of African traditions of expressivity." Joined are the imperative of innovation and the persistence of the diasporic African. Let me say right now that Aldon Nielsen confuses me when he says "African traditions of expressivity" like I am supposed to know what that means. Yes: speaking of black music, *the* Music, Baraka contributes to a strain of aesthetic theory that insists upon black poetry's immanent modernity—its natural closeness to practicing radical critique of the foundational—as black essence, which leads to the "totalizing" Nielsen objects to in Baraka's work. And no: a logic that makes it possible to say "African traditions of expressivity" as if, specifically in relation to aesthetic practices that have come to be identified with local varieties of New World blackness (at any of the several levels at which such a thing might be said to exist, ranging from "styles" of hat and coat-wearing, to styles of playing a brass instrument or singing or singing/dancing, to indeed, ways of speaking/writing), when straining to represent the African, modernity breaks out inside a person; the modern, the black inside a person breaks things, and that breakage becomes the signal of the necessity of breaking that expresses the tie to Africa.

It is not easy to talk about what happens to a person immersed in black culture and life, as I am, as Nielsen has been, as Baraka was (he *was*), to whom the reality of black difference is undeniable (where claiming that black difference is real is also a claim about *orientation*, and also a claim about the way things come to be known) when explanations of blackness' overdetermination appear to come apart at the seam along which everyone agrees the logic of blackness, which cannot be said to be any one thing except originating with the idea of the value of the "African," shall cohere. For me, it has come apart along the seam of the Music. It has come apart because I cannot hold the idea of innovation and the idea of tradition in my mind at the same time without thinking, but how does black writing take place if it is subject to the rigors of never resting? What would a recording of ideas, so punctilious, so exact, a writing without precedent or following, become? Is it possible to read a writing that never rests? How is it possible to get and *stay* between words? What other substance is there, that makes things things, that would make being between words *experience*, however it is possible to understand the limits of possible experience, however it is possible to be things at their limits? Does the unapproachable demand to discover what is between elemental conditions of experience fall on me because of the ways in which blackness, for the sake of its own survival, has been unable to allow the notion of innovation to take an air that is both necessary if it is to remain useful and coherent, and, at the same time, taboo? Innovation cannot claim rest for itself, as black? Not to celebrate, but to see the changes.

What we talk about when we talk about Baraka is the radical "betweenness" of the black, the power of our difference as both righteously motivating essential cause and devastating essential effect. Maybe Nielsen's complaint isn't actually with Baraka's totalizing. Nielsen himself is a tireless advocate for recognizing what he calls "black theory," and it seems to me that that thing, as theory, requires a variety of conceptualizing structures that, orthodox though the concepts may be, make passage for that which cannot be captured. Not to say, then, that there is no such thing as being in the tradition of being African in the New World—a condition of culture that involves what might be called receptivity and appreciation of particular emotions or ideas recognizable in certain expressive manners. This is what we mean when we refer to "black social life." But how to describe these moves, these conditions of culture, when traditions ought not be thought—as Raymond Williams cautions—so as to reinforce "a sense of predisposed continuity"? Mostly, I'm concerned with the implications for contemporary black music, black writing and black life of becoming involved with a featureless "invention" or "innovation" as the main identifier of "African traditions of expressivity"; the implications for movement beyond; the implications for the space and time occupied by contemporary blackness by virtue of the call to innovate in the tradition. And so, finally, we arrive at Mackey.

Mackey on Harris, from Mackey's influential "Sound and Sentiment, Sound and Symbol," where some of the key concepts underlying his magisterial novels are written out:

> *The Angel at the Gate* offers a musical conception of the world whose emphasis on animate incompleteness, "unfinished being," recalls Zuckerlandl's analysis of tonal motion:
> > A series of tunes is heard as motion not because the successive tones are of different pitches but because they have different dynamic qualities. The dynamic quality of a tone, we said, is a statement of its incompleteness, its will to completion. To hear a tone as a dynamic quality, as a direction, a pointing, means hearing at the same time beyond it, beyond it in the direction of its will, and going toward the expected next tone. Listening to music, then, we are not first in one tone, then in the next and so forth. We are rather, always between the tones, on the way from tone to tone; our hearing does not remain with the tone, it reaches through it and beyond it…pure betweenness, pure passing over.

A mixed, middle ground that privileges betweenness would seem to be the realm in which Harris works. He alludes to himself as a "no man's land writer" at one point and later has Jackson say, "I must learn to paint or sculpt what lies stranded between earth and heaven." … [Harris] probes an estrangement and a stranded play in which limbs have to do with limbo, liminality lift[.] … What remains to be said is that to take that lift a bit further is to view the outsider's lot as cosmic, stellar. Social estrangement is gnostic estrangement and the step from Satchmo's "height of trumpet" to Sun Ra's "intergalactic music" is neither a long nor an illogical one. *[my emphasis]*

Mackey's work, like Harris', sets out to become stranded in "betweenness"—"no man's land" "stranded between earth and heaven," "between sky and earth." I'm interested in *From a Broken Bottle Traces of Perfume Still Emanate* as a physical and intellectual practice of "pure passing over" via a poetics that *suspends innovation*—to propose the nature in language of the relation to *this which it is near and that which it is near,* in its betweenness. The practice is of elevating to cosmic status the estrangement between what is heard in the space between one word and another. We are to understand this as a form of radicalism with respect to one's attitude about life's possibilities, insofar as those possibilities are brought about through the orchestration of meanings between each word and others. Fred Moten recognizes this rocking effect as one also theorized by Jacques Derrida.

I am interested in *how* "the good Dr. combines the material social world with and as the origins of Art. The Earth & Sky."

Between the earth and sky, art occurs or originates, begins to become an order in combination with the material/social/world. Art is the work or labor of (the) living, those who are stranded between earth and sky; some*thing* that is made from an essentially space situation, getting on from nowhere to nowhere. And the question really does become, What is it called, what we do that becomes "lived experience?" In the art case, The Case of Blackness is not cosmically unlike any other lived experience. All being in the same condition of mute powerlessness. The Earth & Sky. ("Language beckons us, at first and then again at the end, toward a thing's nature.") What is it called?

I am writing this in the sharpness of the days after Baraka's death, after the deluge of tribute-writing, to get behind or get in front of the essential irreconcilability of our own lived experience and the loss of Baraka's voice, which, for twenty years longer than I have been alive, named Music the poetic dwelling of blacks, how black people fill up space between earth and sky (materially, socially). The *Music*, for Baraka, is a manner or style of responding to the call to name the things among which we are, the organization of space and time as an identifiably black reality. On this view, any and all other blackness remains *in dialogue with the image* of the Music's working out of the following:

Blackly, one dwells in a situation where language not only generally has the jump on you (and you better not forget it) but the jump has caused a further, material/social rift to open up so that you might find yourself in a space that is and is not the space between earth and sky; it is a crease, a fucked up wrinkle, a fold in the already cosmic yawn where it's already impossible to say what the nature of a thing is or might be because *multiplicity and overlap condition the existence of the space*. The dynamism of the lived experience of the black, as she turns this way and that in relation to this and that in relation to the larger spaces in which she is materially constrained, is analogous to that which is "on the way," to the extent that black human being is, also, on its way.

> Many thousands rise and go
> many thousands crossing over
>
> 	O mythic North
> 	O star-shaped yonder Bible city
> Some go weeping and some rejoicing
> some in coffins and some in carriages
> some in silks and some in shackles
> 	Rise and go or fare you well

Music and poetry (music as poetry or the other way round) carry us; they "rise and go."

Before Baraka died, somebody like me, just another stranger, could hear Kenneth Warren's claim that "one can no longer write African-American literature" as an annoying (if transparently provocative) reduction of the proposition (as philosophy) that there is a thing that is blackness, and a poetic project or tradition of identifying the "asymptotic, syncopated nonconvergence(s)" of "event, text and tradition," "Africa, Europe, and America," "outness, labor and sentiment." Now, in part because of Baraka's death and the unfillable hole it opens in the communal practice of this thought, nothing seems more important than getting some understanding about whether one can, or does (any longer), write African-American literature, upon which depends a) the flow of future language relating to the space inside the space between earth and sky that has been called being black, b) the sense of built space around the thing, what it will be called, how language beckons toward it. Now that he is dead. He wrote:

> Blues and bebop are musics. They are understandable, emotionally, as they sit: without the barest discussion of their origins. And the reason I think this is that they are origins, themselves. Blues is a beginning. Bebop, a beginning. They define other varieties of music that come after them. [...]

The roots, blues and bop, are emotion. The *technique*, the ideas, the way of handling the emotion. And this does not leave out the consideration that certainly there is pure intellect that can come out of the emotional experience and the rawest emotions that can proceed from the ideal apprehension of any hypothesis. The point is that such displacement must exist as instinct.

How far are we from the death of Miles, now that Baraka is dead?

[What happens when the improvisation of Enlightenment or modernism or (the philosophy of) (the end of) philosophy—as predicated on the eradication of a certain obsession with differentiated, representative, and representational identity—is lost? What chance does music, the music of the poem, the music that prompts the poem, the music that is prompted by the poem, give us to arrive at such an improvisation? How is such an improvisation to be recalled if its source grows more and more remote, separated from us by the death, by the distance of Miles?]

Between Earth & Sky. Mackey is a votary of betweenness as a specific condition characteristic of being on the outside—the condition, for example of the orphan(ed)—that touches off pursuit of the "most ontic, unheard-of music…ever made."

I'm not suggesting that "African traditions of expressivity" in use today among diasporic Africans, especially in black music, have not, historically, disproportionately constituted the socio-political and aesthetic meaning of outside. (The marginality of the black is, for me, a kind of open-ended truism that this essay isn't about; this essay does not presuppose that and isn't about it.) Yet or still, I've been pointing to the in-between as it has been in use as a philosophical base from which any or all realities come to be articulated. This is the perspective, I've been hinting, of Heidegger in "…Poetically Man Dwells…" where [in the realm of sheer toil] man is allowed to look up, out of it, through it, toward the divinities. The upward glance passes aloft toward the sky, and yet it remains below on the earth. The upward glance spans the between of sky and earth. This between is measured out for the dwelling of man. We now call the span thus meted out the dimension. This dimension does not arise from the fact that sky and earth are tuned toward one another. Rather, their facing each other itself depends on the dimension. Nor is the dimension a stretch of space that is ordinarily understood; for everything spatial, as something for which space is made, is already in need of the dimension, that is, that into which it is admitted. The nature of the dimension is the meting out—which is lightened and so can be spanned — of the between: the upward to the sky as well as the downward to earth. We leave the nature of the dimension without a name.

Nathaniel Mackey knows this. Baraka's interest in Heidegger's way of talking about being (Johannes Koenig) is known to me because Fred Moten has written about it. Moten's engagement with Heidegger's essays on poetry and aesthetics has been indispensable to me for figuring out why how/black people are involved in the philosophical tradition of theorizing our epic staggering around in the space between dust and dust; the infinitely miraculous marvel that it is to make a single expressive grunt or moan or black mark upon a wall: to look up; to feel emotion, to be prompted to arrive at an origin of art, by turning the mind toward the dimension, which Heidegger urges us to consider as neither up nor down but the orienting presence into which thought is groping.

A lot of motherfuckers say almost exactly the same words about the philosophically oriented gesture that is willful cutting into what exists "between earth and sky," heaven and earth, sky and earth. (Emerson, too: his typical prostration in awareness of the impulse to drop a pin: "Where do we find ourselves? In a series of which we do not know the extremes, and believe that is has none?") When I ask, *even if* th Music has come to be understood as a powerful iconography, accumulated over hundreds of years of making, that represents awareness of necessary disjuncture and heads toward (near- or almost-) articulation of betweenness that is black (historical) difference/ways of life, how and why do we speak of it as *indelibly marked by* and always carrying an African study of the repetitive, inscriptive drive toward the center/between (digging) that is always being called "innovation"? (A possible way of life: the *must* of breaking away from the ordinary way of seeing/being seen. Widespread adoption of notions of fugitivity as related to ways of surviving outside the proper, as Mackey, Moten, Judith Butler, and others say, attest to the continuing appeal (regardless of the passage of time and the pastness of the middle passage, slavery, and Jim Crow) of/to a necessary alternative way of knowing the world, like the blacks have done, as a political heuristic that can be made radical.

I'm asking, is it possible to speak of a black musical tradition as that which *alone* makes and follows the way of knowledge, however circuitous, about the significance of the human practice of pointing beyond, specifically, *proper freedom*, however practiced (what techniques, what ideas—the "seemingly endless need for deliberate and agitated rhythmical contrast" "endless changing of direction; stops and starts" "jaggedness" "honking" "timbral effects" "imitation of the human voice"? Beyond what is given or said in the ordinary course of black consignment to toil, deprivation and sociopolitical depression toward what is "ontic and unheard-of" and is, therefore, exactly a move to name the dimension that causes black persons to come into existence with the advent of modernity, and to come into other existences, again and after, with modernity's ebb and flow?

Even if black music does the work a certain now-orthodox way of thinking says it does—and it does—what remains unresolved, anxiety-provoking (I complain of it as a tension, but it is a rub, an ill-fit) is that it seems to me that the set of solutions achieved or achievable musically as black music in America is inextricably linked to a more general gnosticity that has nothing whatsoever to do with blackness, nothing whatsoever to do with a set of "emotions" that are, unquestionably, linked to black life. As Fred Moten suggests in the words I am repeating and repeating ("What happens when the improvisation of Enlightenment is lost...What chance does the music give us to arrive at such an improvisation...if its source grows more and more remote, separated from us by the death, by the distance of Miles?"), we have got to reach some kind of understanding of the interdependence of the projects of general philosophical reaching —thought—and the project of black freedom or we are not going to rightly understand either one. We are not going to continue to be able to describe the mechanisms or routes by which the discovery of breakdown(s) in "the improvisation of Enlightenment" (which I value) converge and diverge in the experience of actual human beings if we cannot see how our chance to get into the posture of arrival at-edge or at- possibility-inconceivable-intheorderofthe-orthodox is not, is no longer, initiated by the practices of thinking upon which we have relied? The contested, fraught nature of black folks' thought and the spectacle that our thinking is, witnessed as art or buffoonery, makes it more and more crucial to continuously revisit the question of what is or has been lost in both the case of the generally gnostic drive and the terrible distance from the emotions that seemed, at one time, to justify themselves as "roots" with respect to this other project: the project of voicing a rejoinder to the captivity of the black who was thought as located in virtually *another dimension*. (Articulation also of the mechanisms by which these projects have been and are joined, which falls to us in consequence of our putative isolation, cause for the sense of desperate peeping [peeping that also defies the laws of light in terms of what can be sign outside an illuminated or enlightened path] that might also attend Baraka's use of the "periscopic" to characterize the visions of black persons as both ingenious and inspired.)

Let Heidegger's formulation of the human relation with space-in-life represent one alluring variant of the general gnosticity; let the Mackey/Harris postmodern recuperation of Dogon cosmology (taken up, too, by Baraka) represent another; Baraka's articulation of emotion or instinct that defines "roots" expression (his recuperation of Du Bois, too, for this purpose: "How does it feel to be *the problem of feeling?*" (my emphasis), yet another.

We have seen fit to name the dimension, "the Music." I refuse Heidegger the position of primary interlocutor with respect to betweenness.

I am, also, "attuned to a gulf between sky and earth." I have understood the poem "music, the music of the poem, the music that prompts the poem, the music that is prompted by the poem" as the site of working out a general gnosticity—what Baraka is getting at when he writes of the emotional situations that non-verbal improvisation arises from, what Moten is talking about in his writing on Cecil Taylor as an unnameable combination of necessary and insufficient tools that do not quite arrive at the reality Taylor witnesses via the *"(work art ritual performance music poetry),"* what Mackey conceptualizes anthropologically in terms of "discrepant engagement" whereby the word that is made creaks with the effort of its being wrought/weaved, all of which seem to me to capture a demand to voice the name, first, of feeling feeling, the first feeling, which is to engage by way of the imagination with an original-type spiritual reality which speaks to a problem of being caught in the terror of between as a material archetype and workhorse of that terror, an experience which is owed black people and has, at a certain cosmic level (the level of the fold, or its unfolding) come to be "owned" by us. Is this our space for taking the measure of ("no mere gauging with ready-made measuring rods for the making of maps")?

We are HERE.

☼

Black Wadada

When it came time for me to say something about *From a Broken Bottle Traces of Perfume Still Emanate*, I got excited about N.'s "post-explanatory" letter dated "17.VII.82," in *Atet A.D.*, a letter in which N. ventures to explain to his pen pal the Angel of Dust what "the balloons are." This letter is, then, a philosophical fragment: a fragment, too, of the novel's thereafter becoming more and more meditation on the unexpected (improvised and also otherworldly) outcome that is the convergence of what is seen and what is heard by way of the thought balloons given off (emanated) by the music of "Djband," variously/progressively called the Deconstructive Woodwind Chorus, East Bay Dread Ensemble, Mystic Horn Society, Molimo m'Atet. I thought I could frame up my exploratory tack (this is a keyword in *From a Broken Bottle*, meaning, sort of, *strategically to approach*) epigraphically ("epigraph" is a more important, perhaps the most important, keyword), by bringing the whole letter into the field of this essay as quotation. I came to this approach only after wishing for a digital, and therefore searchable, version of Mackey's sprawling fiction that would allow for easy compilation and quasi-systematic analysis of the novel's accumulating vocabulary. In the course of things, I had been listening to Eric Dolphy's "The Madrig Speaks, The Panther Walks" (because N./Mackey insists upon its expository relevance) on YouTube. Imagine my disappointment when a random click on the same search term ("The Madrig Speaks") revealed or re-emphasized my general belatedness: I forgot that Fred

Moten has already written about "17.VII.82," working it through a pretty massive formation of statements that coil around Derrida's insight into the breakdown of philosophy's capacity to address "the musical flourish of your own unreadable history," which pertains to the question of how to improvise in the presence of what has already been recorded. Moten finds among the twists in the (logic of) road that leads Derrida back to Algeria the conclusion: "What one receives as a result of indirect, interminable returning to what one already had is a language of feeling that is broached in an emotionally charged, personal and politico-historical insistence." In the balloons,

> Rigorously un/captured, captured but you can't capture it again, heard after the fact of its disappearance, the music—organization in the improvisation of principles, nonexclusion of sound in the improvisation (through the relation and opposition of the generation and subversion) of meaning—lies before us.

(That forgetfulness is so much a counterpart of reading, that forgetting exercises untold power over a text-that-is-being-written, is so obvious. Probably, forgetfulness is the wrong word because what's actually at stake when I lament the inevitable lapse and incapacity that accompanies the work of writing is precisely denial of the repetitious tread of eternal first steps that moved me to write this essay in the first place. Let me pretend that I climb the stair though I do not know the extremes and have no unit with which to measure ascent—that there is no bridge, that there is no advance; that all I have is a beginning. I lift my leg, it breaks; I forget that it is broken and lift again. They call it dance ["adaptive dance," as in A.D.], but it is shambles. Is this the language of feeling to which Moten refers?) I want to forget Moten's probably definitive reading of how "the balloons are" an improvised solution to the permanent problem of being agentically present and simultaneously "uncaptured," and forget to accept that he has recorded Cecil Taylor saying, "the player advances to ... an unknown totality, made whole through self-analysis (improvisation)" so I can return to the place I wanted to go, so it becomes possible to continue thinking about how the fold or crease might be as useful a metaphor as any other, if the object is to find some image that can hold the feeling that one is under extreme pressure to move toward understanding how life can begin to take place where black people are concerned; some whole understanding of the space inside which individual black life (continuously unfolding expression) can take place, not in defiance of opposing powers, but paying them no mind, remaining nonetheless attuned to their structuring presence.

I just want to know what else might be available. What metaphor, if not the Music, will hold the pressure of being forced into "bone-deep listening," uncanny attunement to the surround ("Sometimes you are afraid to listen to this lady")? Do the balloons approach such a metaphorical alternative in spite of their status as tied-off musical emanations that happen because

> You descend into the depths of the music and linger there, dancing in the hoped-for shadow of a bridge, unfathomable ocean song, uncrossable river suite, sentimental avant-garde, subjunctive sentimental mood.

Is this critical approach, where (for Moten) 17.VII.82 stands for a feat of imagination (Mackey's) that succeeds in thinking an instance of having recorded a visible change in previousness that changes or moves the place at which critique begins to take place/invent itself—where the balloons stand for appearance that makes instantaneous sense of action-realized (all that we can hope for?) more than a blip; that causes human action to *begin to record itself as a different thing, ontologically*—therefore foreclosed? Is it closed to me? Can I, do I, get to where Moten already was, where Mackey was, by following the course/cause of the balloons? Is it possible to go there and still be said to be *advancing thinking* about the question of how black innovation, literary and otherwise, is unprofitably tied up (hung up) on metaphors of musical improvisation?

Let me step back. When I said that I wanted to think about the "accumulating vocabulary" of *From a Broken Bottle,* I was alluding to Ian Baucom's phrase (closely linked to the historical poetics of Édouard Glissant) "Time does not pass, it accumulates"; I was wondering how the idea of hauntological time compares with the time of the tense of "wouldly." I was thinking of the tense of Moten's observation in "The Case of Blackness" which is a thought balloon in the universe of my lived reality:

> [A black ontology of disorder…] *will have had to have* operated as a general critique of calculation even as it gathers diaspora as an open set—or as an openness disruptive of the very idea of set—of accumulative and unaccumulable differences, differings, departures without origin, leavings that continually defy the natal occasion in general even as they constantly bespeak the previous. This is a Nathaniel Mackey formulation whose full implications *will have never been fully explorable.* [my emphasis]

And I was thinking of the neologistic employment of "namesake" throughout *From a Broken Bottle.*

1. Readers of *From a Broken Bottle* first encounter the term "namesake" in the first of the series of discourses titled "The Creaking of the Word" where it appears to mean something like a lengthy quote with *genealogical significance.* The discourses themselves are one of several forms of writing that interrupt the primarily epistolary conceit of *From a Broken Bottle*—including dreams recorded-in-writing, poems, dateless letters, "compressed accompaniments," and of course, the *balloons.* (Those forms as *writing* should be distinguished

from the various postures of musical composition, playing music and describing the playing of music even where the written forms seem to emerge from the necessities of being in the presence of musical impulses.) The "Creaking of the Word" is described by N. as both "metalecture" and variously voiced versions/"*virgins*" (fresh, unspoiled versions of the main form from the points of view of various members of "Djband," or, proposals of virgin authorship, after-the-fact of the invention of the form, à la *taking one's solo*) of "after-the-fact lecture/libretto." Let the "fact" be *experience*. "Namesake" consistently performs a kind of predicating function for *Epigraph, Recollection, Anecdote, Exclamation, Encyclical, serenade, ensemble, fluidity* ...

2. "Namesake," therefore, has to be understood as a primary or orienting sign in one of the deep logico-allusive structures of the novel; it is a concept. It begins to appear in the novel, formally, in the context of *libretto*, so it is directly linked with Mackey's development of the idea of the operatic, which comes into play via N.'s interest in Ernst Krenek's "Is Opera Still Possible Today." N. quotes Krenek (where quotation nominates Krenek's essay a namesake text):

> So in modern opera music is not merely a means of heightening, ennobling verbal language—it is not there to make the words more eloquent, so to speak; it is deliberately contrasted with the words, placed behind the words, making them transparent so that you can see their second inner significance. ... The music does not achieve this by "heightening" the words but by opening an abyss of meaning and countermeaning behind them.

Without the idea of the operatic, or, the language-vision that is produced via the lens of opera, that is, *opera glass*, we can't fully understand or approach matters related to a subjectivity that is both transparent and glass-like, tending to break, that figure throughout the novel (the Broken Bottle of the title; Jarred Bottle [he of the fractious name, "whose names were legion"]: J.B., J&B, Flaunted Fifth, DB, Djbot Baghostus; the I/eye "made of opera glass"; the "glass-bottom boat"). Opera stands for creative conditions under which glass-like subjectivity *can articulate* antithesis, "taking the ending of pretenses as the basic intention of a new style." Operatic conditions are the historical groundwork upon which improvisation of the "ontic and unheard (of)" music of the future depends.

The opera of the future, for which "The Creaking of the Word" serves as libretto, is the first work of a new music-of-the-word composed against or without the necessity of wordlessness, given as a primary feature of the orthodox/traditional music and the *sine qua non* of its "presumed elevation." The harmony the new music proposes between music and the (written) word might declare the sound of instruments—"acousticality"—superfluous, but only where superfluousness is attributable to the fact of having been composed in an attitude of "deep-listening," in contemplation of a vast and growing archive of music (N. is always referring to contemporary [1970s and 1980s] releases of new recordings; see *From a Broken Bottle*'s Discography), mostly diasporic black music, *mostly* jazz. This music is *part of* the text in a way that is only partly analogous to the relation of the libretto to the acoustic element of an opera in ways that I want to deal with more thoroughly later. For now, it has to be noted that the opera for which "The Creaking of the Word" is being written, is being written in an attitude of responsiveness to music beyond any layperson's sense of the phenomenology of listening (like Jean-Luc Nancy's *Listening*). The writing takes place in a DMZ of "sound and sight rolled into one," which is the territory of **deranged subjectivity**, the magical space in which it is possible for the formation of the balloons to become lived reality.

3. Hotel Didjeridoo is a monument, although a monument/museum

in the sense that even Wynton Marsalis protests against when he says that jazz is not a museum music. When, in *Atet A.D.*, N.'s *wouldly* opera foretells the downfall of Hotel Didjeridoo, the (whore) House of Jazz & Blues, we're to understand the downfall of that imaginary house of the traditional music as no less than a revolutionary rejection of the logic of a certain black tradition, which is a logic or theory of history (a system for arranging time in terms of value) in favor of the elaboration of namesake time, the time of *wouldly*, called also "post-expectant," in which the new tradition must take shape alongside breakdown, as collapse, foregoing the romantic fantasy of permanent wholeness, of *permanence*. (In this case the permanent legibility of blackness, so closely linked with black creativity, via historical practices of blues and jazz.) Thus, Djamilaa expresses the whole number 4 as a "roundabout fraction"—[6 squared over 21/7 squared]—"cracking the consistency of the whole," a move that is consistent with the way the definitional weight of the "operatic" on one hand controls the structure of and on the other recedes in to the background of an improvised transcript of the "opening of an abyss of meaning and countermeaning behind" the notion of the operatic.

4. Namesake Epigraph #1 came from a book on the Dogon:

> 'The word,' said the old man, 'is the sound of the block and the shuttle. The name of the block means "creaking of the word." Everybody understands what is meant by "the word" in that connection. It is interwoven with the threads; it fills the interstices in the fabric.'

There is already *anaphora* to describe how epigraph works. Putative reinvention of the critical frame does not automatically require a responsive act of invention, as radical. Maybe I just repeat. Recall Baraka's commentary on the nature of Cecil Taylor's genius, which was at the same time traditional and magical/fresh. But I feel like I have to come again, with something new, at the problem of the epigraphic frame for *From a Broken Bottle*, if only because I feel pressed to do so in order to gesture toward some kind of feminine understanding of "interstices" or "cut," *sexual cut* ["'Sexual' comes into it only because the word 'he' and the word 'she' rummage about it in the crypt each defines for the other, reconvening as whispers at the chromosomal level as though the crypt had been a crib, a lulling mask, all along. In short, it's apocalypse I'm talking about, not courtship."], through which rub/apocalyptic play becomes the site of the emergence or manufacture of subject-initiating word(s)-for-reality.

I'm interested in what fresh epistemological satisfactions arise when physical/spatial (which might be the absence of or the condition for primarily "material" ideologies of black personhood), as opposed to sonic/linguistic (not that this is an exposé of the "seeing-said" as just another used-to-be useful dialectic), aspects of thinking the difference between black art traditions and any other kinds of tradition come forward by way of repeating/writing-down/re-reading as a method of placing oneself in contact with or over top of the physical space that has been occupied by a previous text. This writing in order to be with is not directed toward the production of the palimpsest, which implies willed dumbness or dimness, scribbling over the substantive previousness—part limitation, part condition of possibility—that must at some level be the subject of the writing, that to which the writing becomes subject and to which the subject's criticality comes to pass in the presence of. That is, it is the fact of *the writing that is there already* that matters, not the fact of its removal, illegibility, or the act of squeezing into a space of legibility that remains in order to make one's authorship visible.

Barely, I am able to discern that Fred Moten's critical actions with respect to the balloons double down on the anaphoric as a way of systematizing relation-back. Moten knows that the balloons exist symbolically along the way ("with but not of") to propositions that answer the question, *How does it feel to be the problem of feeling?* So, he lets 17.XI.82 bring up the rear in a series of long quotations dealing with the question of what exactly Eric Dolphy was saying on record, in his performances, for example with Charles Mingus, what he said as a matter of record, which is the only way we have of knowing what problems of feeling became manifest in the sounds he made. The balloons double down, therefore, on the question of what namesake is—Moten reading Mackey reading innovation (what comes to pass in an instant or present, what is preserved as "remainder" in the instant) in light of previousness, in light of what has been previously written, in light of what "the balloons are," in light of what they record *of historical feeling.* "This is the history. This is your history, my history, the history of the Negro People," are grandiloquent words Baraka puts in the mouth of Sterling Brown, who he remembers holding forth to him and A. B. Spellman on the cultural value of Brown's record collection.

With "The Creaking of the Word" libretti and the grander logic of the operatic, Mackey invokes music and alludes to the manner in which black history is inflected by it, but leaves music in a complex relation with the worldview that comes into being through Mackey's work. For me, Djband's black/cross-cultural, truly cosmic—or, he says, "ontic,"—music threatens the independent spiritual and professional intellectual significance of traditional notions of black music. The great fear that results from buying into an operatic/ontic namesake logic would be that "blues" as shorthand for black aesthetic difference—its condition and reason-for-being—would become dislodged from its backhanded pedestal by accurately describing its truly contemporary function as genuine only in the extent to which it demonstrates the phenomenon of super-cultural, corporatized erasure of the lived reality of black persons.

As Mackey puts it in an interview with Jeanne Heuving:

> [The appeal of experimental or avant-garde approaches] is that they bring a critical, questioning frame of mind to bear on artistic precepts, particularly conventional or accepted practices and ideas. Their inspiration, one could say, is the undoing or dismantling of the inflated status those practices and ideas may have come to have. Samuel Beckett, at a certain moment, for example, steps in and strips the theater of a certain over investment in realist notions of dialogue and set design. These approaches nonetheless run their own risks of inflation.

Mackey remains the best commentator on his own work.

5. *From a Broken Bottle Traces of Perfume Still Emanate* is important to me because it enacts a thoroughly gripping examination of possible convergence and divergence between the possibilities proposed for black personhood by way of performing and listening to music (that is, of music-based theories of radical black personhood) and possibilities proposed by way of writing. I can't shake the intuition that with these four books Nathaniel Mackey does the impossible by insisting on the correctness of the music-based theory while accessing a poetics that permanently destabilizes all its premises. With *From a Broken Bottle*, Nathaniel Mackey ruins the intention to run-on indefinitely with a poetics that is simultaneously music-based, black and radical—ruins it forever.

N. and the band play an expansive and highly experimental music in the jazz tradition (and that's complicated), and inspired by each member's meditations on how to advance in the music and how to make spiritual advances in freedom. Mackey allows for and then maximizes (or maxes out) the use of what I call the trope of the "up and out," part of a familiar poetic discourse of ascent/descent—the discourse that gives us "Way Out West," "Out to Lunch," "Air"

"Ascension" "Interstellar Space" Sun-Ra and George Clinton. Balloons given off (Mackey's word is "emanated") by the music of N. and the band arguably put words in the mouth of the player, as he thinks about and makes music that communicates his reflections upon what to do/how to live, and because they are balloons, the words float away, float off and out. One of the band's members puts it this way: "It's not about being here anymore. I've gotta tighten up my concept, give it a few turns I've gotta go elsewhere to get." Reading this novel, readers assent to an absolute weave between playing to live a new life and living to play a new music, playing live and playing life: we assent to the invention of a "realm" (Mackey's word from *Bass Cathedral*) in which the thought/action divide is taken to be a bunch of baloney. Subjectivity problem #1 for black aesthetics solved: Mackey's fictional black people don't have to argue for the political significance of acts of art because the order of politics recedes behind the cosmic order that controls events, such as the manifestation of thought balloons. (Or, bring on a politics of this derangement.) In so far as he solves this perennial problem of feeling, this novel is a work of genius and a masterpiece.

The objective is that, for me, language that *goes off* doesn't aspire to the condition of music; it aspires to itself. What's fascinating in *From a Broken Bottle* is that the massive scale and complexity of the changes-in-self Mackey envisions for his fictional black persons might (and I can't imagine that he doesn't know this) require them to give up a sacredly held view of their central spiritual and intellectual ritual—playing music. This is why the balloons are such a HUGE PROBLEM. This is why they take over the narrative; this is why, after their first appearance, the novel becomes more and more meditation on the unexpected (improvised and also otherworldly) outcome that is the convergence of what is seen and what is heard by way of the aesthetic rupture or break that coincides with the appearance of the balloons. If the novel is actually playing out, as I think it is, a scene whereby music is decentered by an alternative thought tradition—a newfangled black gnostic poetics—then the writer of the novel and its readers are left in the awkward position of having narrowed the possibilities for relating to those who are not actually, currently participating in the poetic practices of reading/ writing/listening that the novel simultaneously invents and operates prophetically on behalf of. Again, re-newing the central problem of the avant-garde, and also undermining the orthodox principles of a given avant-garde. And who wants to be the John the Baptist of black people?

Moving self-consciously to displace the centrality of 17.VII.82 as the text that tells "what the balloons are," then, here it is, N.'s initial take on the problem from the third book of the novel, *Atet, A.D.*

> The balloons are words taken out of our mouths, an eruptive critique of predications rickety spin rewound as endowment. They subsist, if not on excision, on exhaust, abstract-extrapolative strenuousness, tenuity, technical-ecstatic duress. They advance the exponential potency of dubbed excision—plexed, parallactic articulacy, vexed elevation, vatic vacuity, giddy stilt. They speak of overblown hope, loss's learned aspiration, the eventuality of see-said formula, filled-in equation, vocative imprint, prophylactic bluff. They raise hopes while striking an otherwise cautionary note, warnings having to do with empty authority, habitable indent, housed as well as unhoused vacuity, fecund recess.

> The balloons are love's exponential debris, "high-would'" atmospheric dispatch. Hyperbolic aubade (love's post-expectant farewell), they arise from the depth we invest in ordeal, chivalric trauma—depth charge and buoy rolled into one. They advance an exchange adumbrating the advent of optic utterance, seen-said exogamous mix of which the coupling of tryst and trial would bear the inaugural brunt. Like Djeannine's

logarithmic flute, they obey, in the most graphic imaginable fashion, ocular deficit's oracular ricochet, seen-said remit.

The balloons are thrown-away baggage, oddly sonic survival, sound and sight rolled into one. They map even as they mourn post-appropriative precincts, chthonic or subaquatic residua come to the surface caroling world collapse. They dredge vestiges of premature post-expectancy (overblown arrival, overblown goodbye), seen-said belief's wooed risk of inflation, synaesthetic excess, erotic-elegiac behest. The balloons augur—or, put more modestly, acknowledge—the ascendancy of videotic premises (autoerotic tube, autoerotic test pattern), automatic stigmata bruited as though of the air itself.

The balloons are one sign in a whole Mackey-an symbolic world, one small piece of one deep logico-symbolic structure of sound/sight meditation in a novel that is unbearably dense with deep logico-symbolic structures— no "meta" reading suggests itself because each symbolic structure vies with, informs, contradicts, another. The operatic, the post-expectant, the phoneme Dj-.

The balloons are impossible to understand, philosophically. From a Broken Bottle warns against the folly of approaching this language that is exhaust with "formula," one character wisely concluding that "it's hard to say" what they are—philosophy can't say. But that doesn't mean that "words don't go there," necessarily, even if you can't read words that refuse to become singularly referential; that become, instead, writing made of air, writing that becomes matter.

The balloons speak, to me, anyway, of the stakes involved in moving into the space of "Considering how exaggerated music is," what that might mean, and precisely because I've been warned: THAT WAY MADNESS LIES.

The balloons emerge out of, are synaesthetically coterminous with the energetic and psychological demands (including crippling (mind-fucking) episodes of lost time, unbearable cranial pain, automatic writing, prophetic shared dreams) of composing and performing ACTING in and through unconfirmed dimensions of experience toward "the most ontic music ever heard."

The balloons put a comic quietus on the dead serious performance of the music. The balloons' "rough poetry" wins out over the demand to hear, as sacred sound, the most ontic music ever made. People want to pay to see the magic balloons. Language that goes off doesn't aspire to the condition of music, is unspectacular; it surpasses music's exaggeration by way of new specificity, specificity that highlights discovery and enjoyment of poetic hyper-referentiality achieved via dismemberment/disaggregation of ONE heroic consciousness. In the poem, I become one in conversation with myself and others.

The balloons propose a potent anti-essentialism for which we are not even ready, displacing the black genius improviser as the vector of discovery however much he goes out. This way, this freedom to transform and go out of the body as such, as of the troubles of the past body, is made possible by heroism but does not re-enter it by way of the new thing it makes possible to understand as proper.

The balloons come to pass when we write with knowledge of the possibility of becoming multiple as dreamers of the same dream, when we write a proper writing in-keeping with the multi-layered experience of "deep listening."

The balloons are proper writing. They are a proper cosmic response to an alignment achieved through N.'s libretto of a non-acoustic opera, the unacknowledged scrawl that outs. N.'s/Mackey's powers of composition will out the alignment of performance/listening : playing/memory : speech/playing : conversation/argument taking place in the present by way of an archive that is heavily musical.

N. writes (he says he is "quoting a book on Stravinsky"), "In the Kingdom of the Father there is no drama, but only dialogue, which is disguised monologue." The balloons come to pass at the junction of the namesake epigraph. They pass by anaphora to re-describe how epigraph works. How ancestry works. The balloons change the direction of the address of proper black writing, away from the possibility of its being received by the many, and toward the possibility of its being understood by a few.

The balloons, too, "invoke music" and come into being in a manner that alludes to the ways in which black history is inflected by music, but leaves music in a ambivalent and altered—ambivalent because altered—relation with the worldview that takes music to be at the center of an elaborated black ontology. The great fear would therefore be that "blues" as shorthand for black aesthetic difference would become dislodged from its backhanded pedestal if words were to really go off.

The balloons are an emanation of rage we do not yet know we feel upon encountering conditions of writing that would take us away from sound and into the age of the epigraph.

If there is such a thing as anaphoric history, then the logic of that history is demonstrated and tested by way of epigraphic namesake relation that restlessly rests on a "rickety, crackpot" manner of witness (for Mackey, to make is to make (song), to witness is to hear, or, to listen to what has been interwoven with the fabric of the real). Whereby Namesake Epigraph #1 on the "creaking of the word" is #1 among writings selected to collectively form the aesthetic present. Whereby the similarity of these luminous images comes into play:

Mute-Stereoptic Emanation: B'Loon
(Composite Sketch Based on Eyewitness Accounts)

Paul Gilroy writes, "Thinking about music—a non-representational, non-conceptual form—raises aspects of embodied subjectivity that are not reducible to the cognitive and the ethical." Through the balloons Mackey suggests the contestability (he contests) the view that music is "non-representational, non-conceptual," refusing to perpetuate the split between the literal and the oral that links the course of the history of black aesthetic difference to the history of enlightened reason as a history of terrorizing black persons. The balloons, it seems to me, propose a new logic of black (aesthetic) history that I am calling anaphoric or epigraphic, predicated on the artist's ability to develop a deranged and *hyper-cognitive* understanding of her location on a grid of recordings—textual, somatic, spiritual or what have you. The theoretical place of music here is, at best, indeterminate, conditional upon a person's individual capacity to cognitively and spiritually disengage from certain apparently inescapable "material" conditions; to cause her own escape from what has previously been understood as the history of her own self; to escape from the Music and into a cracked and crackpot multiform kind of practice that, like B'loon, the anthropomorphized figure of the balloons that is the product of N.'s brain-fever induced automatic writing, is "the sign of a strain or struggle to come into being, a fraught, unfinished harbinger of something not yet fully with us, a sign of something yet to come." B'loon is the figure of the wouldly; the Angel of Dust, a friend out of time, his only friendly witness.

☼

Black Wadada

> We want to think about what makes New World slavery what it is in order to pursue that future anteriority which, being both within it and irreducible to it, will have unmade it, and that futurity which always already unmakes it.
>
> — Jared Sexton, "The Social Life of Social Death"

> The club, our subcenobitic thing, our block chapel, is a hard row of improvisational contact, a dispossessive intimacy of rubbing, whose mystic rehearsal is against the rules or, more precisely, is apposed to rule, and is, therefore, a concrete social logic often (mis)understood as nothing but foolishness, which is, on the other hand, exactly and absolutely what it is.
>
> — Fred Moten, "Blackness and Nothingness (Mysticism in the Flesh)"

But there is another approach. Quickly, parallel to the social, spiritual and temporal re-arrangements that the balloons "record" through/ as the art practice of Djband as complete (liberated or liberating) in its blackness, we must keep in mind or rather think at the same time the general conditions that form the boundaries of blackness. These parallel theoretical developments compete and converse with literature to provide terms and, thus, to constitute the relevant contemporary discursive field upon which we think ("anti anti-essentially") about what is and is not a form of black life.

What I have said thus far raises or leaves available to be raised at least three platforms for viewing black intellectual events. First, the question of how the fold/crease/wrinkle/origami thing which certain black (male) intellectuals have invented and theorized as a musical thing, and I'm saying is not, cannot be permanently linked to the actual practice of music and is, rather, a poetic thing that "flashes up" in its contemporary manifestation as the image of the balloons in *From a Broken Bottle*. I'm saying, furthermore, that, as such, this poetic thing is a pretty wonderful claim about the nature of black time-space, black history—how black people have been, are and will be. (The *wouldly* is inscription of the desire for alternative historiographies; the obsessive interest in the future anterior tense tests this desire tentatively ...).

There is also the question of the relation of black intellectual practice as art practice, a practice that desires *folding* as a method of interiorizing the most outside, frequently characterized as the deep, to another critical foray into the mechanics of folding, namely that of Gilles Deleuze. That is, the black critical theory of today is already moving to develop a set of concepts that deal adequately with *post-blackness*, the discernible effects upon a black sense of the world that the postmodern process of dismantling a violently anti-black regime will continue to have. This theory sometimes asks, Is black history a blessing or a curse? When, of course, the question is really, How does each individual black person work the edge of inside and outside that blackness reveals? What resources and alliances for livable life are accessible to her now and (how) do we name as black the multiplicity of these practices at the edge? How is what I'm saying about poetics related to this ecrito-theoretical work? (We must never forget this question: What is literary criticism?)

Finally, I'm going to have to explain how it is that the contemporary Music is true in its bewildering rejection of its own status as the star of a certain kind of radical thinking about getting out or outside. Perhaps it will become possible to think about what kinds of freedom or captivity individual acts (performances, projects, songs) of rejecting that apotheotic status might imply when we look at the Music as it really is today. From these acts, what general statements can be made about how musicians themselves understand the contemporary critical status or position of the self, genre and song? In order to do this, we'll have to say out loud that "the antiphonal accompaniment to gratuitous violence—the sound that can be heard as if in response to that violence, the sound that must be heard as that to which such violence responds" is a sound that includes not only the unassailable music of Miles, but also the assaultive music known as "trap" that takes violence inside itself in a manner that no one could mistake for ironic and, nonetheless, and I guess arguably, remains in conversation with the signal (gnostic) longing for whole life that has been called "freedom drive."

※

Fold Crease Wrinkle

What is power? What is intimacy? How do we know this at all? How to communicate it? And where or when are these questions, and their relation, posed with greater force—political force, psychic force, historical force—than within the precinct of the New World slave estate, and within the time of New World slavery? [...] If the intimacy of power suggests the sheer difficulty of difference, the trouble endemic to determining where the white imagination ends and the black imagination begins, then the power of intimacy suggests, with no less tenacity and no less significance, that our grand involvement across the color line is structured like the figure of an envelope, folds folded within folds: a black letter law whose message is obscured, enveloped, turned about, reversed. Here a structure of violence is inscribed problematically in narrative, an inscription that can only struggle and fail to be something other than a writing-off, or a writing-over.

I have proposed the image of a fold, sometimes substituting "crease" or "wrinkle," to describe an aesthetic practice of desire that is what blackness is, and I have proposed this as an alternative to the image of blackness as a sound, an archive of sound. I'm willing to take it for granted that folding and the idea of folding are elemental in language intending to describe spaces that are brought into contact with other spaces ("rubbing"), and natural also to languages of intimacy and of eros. That is, the way folding is in the air is kind of generic—at least not proprietary—and it may be that I am more interested in the word and action in its ordinary (as opposed to philosophical) sense, but there is a dialogue of the fold specific to the question of how blackness works as a historical relation.

Jared Sexton, in his impassioned essay "The Social Life of Social Death: On Afro-Pessimism and Black Optimism," quoted above, ends up thinking the fold (echoing deep out of Du Bois and probably accidentally crossing over Baraka's encounter with Du Bois' "grandest work," *Black Reconstruction*—or not, or, hiding a citation to that work in Benjaminian style, as I said before, in the orthodox philosophical style, making a claim to originality, which sticks in my craw) as "our grand involvement across the color line ... structured like the figure of an envelope, folds folded within folds"). I am babylike in my reading practice in that I can still be startled by unfamiliar or sudden noises; I startle at the notion of the fold as an image of "our grand involvement across the color line." Grand? What is grand here? Does Sexton mean this word to indicate the temporal scope of "our involvement" or its *volume*, the large space it occupies in the whole of things? Or, having a manner that is self-consciously fancy and ultimately delusional about the intimacy of the intimacy? For, if "involvement across the color line" is a special or specific form of an intimate relation of power, Sexton's statements imply an understanding of the space of racial order as genuinely double-sided (in spite of his own questions about "an untenably strict delimitation of inside and out" that comes about through a faulty understanding of (Moten's terms) "interdiction" and "transgression"). Rather, the crux of the color-line relation is the relation of positions that are genuinely different from each other. Black and white difference is real and reified by Sexton's folding, whose operation moves *the different* together in language ("in narrative") in such a way that they lay atop one another, cover one another, cancel one another ("obscured, enveloped, turned about, reversed"). The unfunny agony of the intimate power relation is the impossibility of being as one—even as the different depend upon one another to differentiate themselves as racialized subjects.

Sexton and Moten are in in dialogue about, let's not forget,—I really want to say this right—the question of whether black life needs a (its own or *specific*) "philosophy of life" in order to fully describe blackness as that modern form of life essentially "associated with a certain sense of decay" (I would add a sense of foreboding), which they undertake to study, most notably, in the work of Franz Fanon— work developed more recently in the U.S. case by Saidiya Hartman, Sexton, Nahum Dimitri Chandler and Frank Wilderson III, among others. These theorists end up contributing to the elaboration of general philosophical principles about the ways in which persons live as objects (or, depending on who you are reading, how certain categories of person outlive historical objecthood), but they do so with the specific understanding that the "case of blackness" /"positionality" of black people emerges *under slavery*; that is, there is agreement about the fact that we are dealing with a form of life that does not exist but for slavery, that slavery is the condition that creates the "lived experience of the black." The critical question becomes, "What does slavery mean for the very conception of the objective pronoun 'us'?", a question Sexton's essay gets to in conversation with Fred Moten's 2008 essay "The Case of Blackness." How are black people to understand their relations with each other through time and space when being in the time and space of "the black" is undeniably to exist as the most wretched, degraded and abject set of beings that ever lived? (But David Walker has a sense of humor.) In the past in the present in the future *what can black people themselves recognize as proper to themselves* as survivors of successive plots to render blackness as living death, wretchedness and thingliness? How will we know our likeness to one another if we are no longer within the slave regime? And, *if* we are no longer there and no longer that (I'm not sure that Hartman accepts this, and I'm not sure whether there is a sharp line of delineation at Jubilee or, say, passage of the Civil Rights Act, for Chandler, Sexton and Wilderson), then are we us no longer? These are weirdly simple questions that precede and lead toward elaboration of "the regulatory metaphysics" of our art as *representation of* a philosophy of life that comes into being because of (let's just say because) what becomes, because of slavery, the color line. The dialogue is also about, as Moten writes, *the environment in which blackness acts and reacts:* "the air of the thing that escapes enframing—an often unattended movement that accompanies largely unthought positions and appositions." The space and spaces where blackness can be perceived to begin and end (in the mind), as Sexton says, are not abstract: they are defined by a succession of hostile racial regimes that aim to crush blackness out of existence.

In the context of the Moten/Sexton dialogue, which I'm declaring an internal, and therefore infolding, critique of the problem of black nothingness—what is the charge, positive or negative, of nothingness?—to speak of folding is to speak of the stakes of distributing black presence and imaginings in the world. What are the effects of that distribution worth? What is being touched by the presence of/ living blacks going to mean? The language of folding thus highlights the encounter between blackness and its outside. What's delightful about Moten's formulation—"the air of the thing that escapes enframing" —naming the surrounds and atmosphere of blackness, is the way he remains agnostic about the delineation of a boundary; he allows the difference of outside blackness to remain faint or dimly perceived. The difference is respiratory, unnoticed. Blackness is its own place, always next to the place where place is thought to begin, whose inside is knowledge of the falseness of, *the defiance of,* enclosure. As in *Black Reconstruction,* leaving that bullshit behind.

[The club, our subcenobitic thing, our block chapel, is a hard row of improvisational contact, a dispossessive intimacy of rubbing, whose mystic rehearsal is against the rules or, more precisely, is apposed to rule, and is, therefore, a concrete social logic often (mis)understood as nothing but foolishness, which is, on the other hand, exactly and absolutely what it is.]

The human condition that defies enclosure, yet requires togetherness, and is "against the rules" Moten suggests, is discoverable, naturally, only in metaphysical/"mystical" "rehearsal" (here comes the music), another word for practice. This condition is always (never) coming to pass, becoming, even in its concrete-ness, even given the evidentiary impact of its constitutive sociality. The covenant that makes our "thing" a thing that can be apprehended is the promise to stay together in the absurd or "foolish" space of the self that accepts itself as black, surrounds itself with blacks, a promise that is made and renewed by a self in "constant improvisational contact" with other facets of the world, organic and inorganic alike: earth and sky and the human and his air. Lingering within Moten's meditation on black life as "our life in the folds" is a poet's sense that the action of black life is not the action of "obscur[ing], envelop[ing], [turning about, reversing]" that Sexton imagines as the characteristic shape or event of racialized "involvement." The rehearsal of which Fred Moten speaks is always going to find its highest expression beyond the explanatory capacity of the fundamentally juridical system of opposition and antagonism that "the color line," or, being to one side or another of the opposition that is the color line, implies. Even if that opposition is understood to be initiated by the basest falsehood backed up by systematic violence and partially constituted by that violence, to say the "color line" conjures, even if I think in terms of the vastness of Du Bois' sense of the material plus the metaphysical remainder, for me, a whole series of thoughts that unhelpfully close the circuit of thinking about oneself. "At stake," Moten writes, "is the curve, the suppleness and subtlety, not of contemplation on social life but of contemplative social life; at stake is the force of an extra-phenomenological poetics of social life." The highest expression of elementary blackness:

> Chant and kōan and moan and Sprechgesang, and babble and gobbledygook, le petit nègre, the little nigger, pidgun, baby talk, bird talk, Bird's talk, bard talk, bar talk, our locomotive bar walk and black chant, our pallet cries and whispers, our black notes and black cant, the tenor's irruptive habitation of the vehicle, the monastic preparation of a more than three-dimensional transcript, an imaginal manuscript we touch upon the walls and one another, so we can enter into the hold we're in, where there is no way we were or are.

This litany alerts us to a key aspect of the liveliness of Moten's work: its theory of blackness prizes nonce description, crowding together epithet character love sound, the illogic and impossibility of the human being "a slave," only to allow for the dissipation of description's momentary accuracy. He aligns himself with the edge of the envelope, as it were, before it is an envelope, where it is all cutting edge and pulp and air and is held and is moving. The analogy in speech is the eruption of "babble and gobbledygook"—the poetic space. You cannot really "inscribe" anything on the surface of flux. You cannot "narrate" a "structure of violence" upon it. There is no way to prove this.

It's unclear, as yet, whether *to fold,* philosophically, when it comes to the black "philosophy of life" of which Sexton and others speak—most notably and searchingly for this discussion, Amiri Baraka in *Black Music*—can mean anything other than to involve oneself in the history of involvement as antagonism and intractable opposition, penetrating to split the ontological fields of antagonists, as Frank Wilderson has it, across the one and only color line.

Also—why do we have to talk like this in order to describe black people's being together? Who cares what Gilles Deleuze said about folding? When I relate back to him through the Sexton-Moten matrix of men's thinking, is that a retrograde act of criticism that strengthens the history of the ownership of all known words by thought that obsessively measures its relation to knowledge that can only be white and male? Black women can't think from Thomas Jefferson right on out to lunch ... What is necessary in the discourse of folding? What caused me to happen upon it? This:

> Why would something be folded, if it were not to be enveloped, wrapped or put into something else? It appears that here [the point at which 'simple intuition' reveals the final cause of the fold] the envelope acquires its ultimate or perhaps final meaning: it is no longer an envelope of coherence or cohesion, like an egg, in the 'reciprocal envelopment' of organic parts. Nor even a mathematical envelope of adherence or adhesion, where a fold still envelops other folds, as in the enveloping envelope that touches an infinity of curves in an infinity of points. It is an envelope of inherence or of unilateral 'inhesion': inclusion or inherence is the final cause of the fold, such that we move indiscernibly from the latter to the former. Between the two, a gap is opened which makes the envelope the reason for the fold: what is folded is the included, the inherent. It can be stated that what is folded is only virtual and currently exists only in an envelope, in something that envelops it.

The color line is "something" that envelops the possibility of becoming folded in black imagination (and that folding is the subject of black critical theory), a necessary and insufficient station on the path of an unfolding form of self insofar as we pass through it—a scrim of fact—as we move nearer to a self-on-its-way. Yet, the color line is not of this world; the color line has no soul and cannot ever inhere in a human being. If we had been in the hold and were never held, we were never, neither, actually excluded by "the black letter of the law," which all along wrote something like the depression of our inclusion as the color line; black subjectivity is the horrible harmony of power and intimacy; the color line is exactly the manifestation of imperial failure to constitute a subjectivity of racialized difference. That which constitutes the subject can be understood to differ from that which comes inside the person insofar as what comes inside is fundamentally organic: the being of which we speak is alive. Let us take the physical limits of the body under investigation somewhat literally when it is time for us to believe in its natural possibility, and not only when it is time to meditate on the various ways in which it has been harmed. The living body is not only a thing/object to which violence can be done. Imagine the "more than three dimensional transcript" of the system of thinking black imagination's possibilities as a live system, soft. Imagine that the color line can never really touch anyone or anything. When we talk about folding, we attempt, I heard Mei-mei Burssenbrugge say, to bring together earth and sky. The discourse of folding is a discourse of relation that touches the actions of bringing together both elements that are infinitely far apart and those that are infinitely close (inherent). When we talk about folding, we gain access to a language of betweenness with tremendous symbolic sweep, language appropriate to figuring blackness as that which is so far from the subject whose objecthood it names. When we think about folding, we give primary attention to something "virtually" perceived, meta/physical notions by way of which it becomes possible to reorganize our notions of interior and exterior (Earth/Sky/Fourfold/the stars). Do you see? Black imagination already is; blackness is a thing whose inherence is partially concealed by the horror that (presently) envelops it.

I don't think it is the case, then, that blackness, even when we take into consideration the distinction between blackness and black subjectivity sometimes made in the developing discourse of black being, can be, as Nahum Chandler proposes, "atopic in the sense that it is outside of spatiality as a given." Indeed, I do not know what it would mean to locate existence outside "spatiality as a given" unless we are ultimately saying something like "the black is outside history as given," true only in the radical and exclusively discursive sense developed by Spillers, Hartman, Wilderson, Chandler, and others. The black is outside time/the black is outside space? How can this be, even if the black is recorded as outside ontology or constructed as a remnant in the language of language so that she is inconceivable in the face of her gore? Here I am, *we are here together,* inside this time-space together. The desire to eradicate me from the frame cannot accomplish its object completely; therefore, the total eradication from being of the black is, by definition, a total failure. The nowness I inhabit is an inherence that rebukes my concealment, the extremity of my inclusion. This is how I have come to understand Spillers' flesh/body distinction: *no you* without the devastation of my body. This modern world folds us together, envelops us in the color line and the discovery of blackness as rending itself, or gap, or inherence is the discovery of the true time: that which is possible at the level of the human at any given instant. What might be or become if we give ourselves over to a theory of that space *that is without history.* This is very hard, both to give oneself over to the now and to theorize its instantaneous continuity.

[…[Foucault] writes a history, but a history of thought as such … Thinking makes both seeing and speaking attain their individual limits, such that the two are the common limit that both separates and links them]

From a Broken Bottle is a text that concerns itself relentlessly with playing out the implications of "an extra-phenomenological poetics of (black) social life," where blackness is an intensification of all known practices of making black music collectively/socially so that the collective practice is thought, as fiction or "a name—a theoretical object—for thought," a background condition for all taking place. Inside this fictional blackness, where N. acknowledges no outside of black thought except via address to the personality of ether, The Angel of Dust/History himself *(outside as anecdote and aside, outside as opera)*, where the limits of the seen/said thrust us into an experience of life that is proposed as "extra-phenomenological" (extra-philosophical, outside a *philosophy of life*) in persistently exceeding the categories supposed to explain human being and within which black personhood would be either confined or negated. What should we say about thinking that is the common limit (separating and linking) of the observable and the spoken? Is organized sound—musicality—necessarily the answer to this question? Isn't a musical "answer" a mere reassertion of the categorical and, therefore, hardly extra-phenomenological? Is it possible to recognize now (about the balloons) that what has been at stake all along in the "subcenobitic thing" that is the Black Music Juggernaut is desire for the disinterment, or rather the illumination, of an aspect of thought that is of the devil—insofar as it describes the unobservable and unheard (of) and allows for communication only via belief in a certain attunement to how it feels to be a problem? What has been at stake all along is a practice of language and writing that formalizes the gesture of agreement to explore—in social life as art practice—an interior that the discourse of the color line does not, cannot, tolerate. The notion of "involvement across the color line" is too much within, as opposed to at the limits of, seeing and speaking at the level of language, such that it cannot permit simultaneity of the qualities of inherence and the qualities of passage beyond that black imagination manifests; thought that circulates, person to person, recognizably, beyond the difference the "color line" inculcates by way of its name. "Future anteriority"=to be free of the color line, having existed all the while by way of its motivation or envelopment.

※

Dear Tom Krell

Sometimes I think I must be mistaken in my apprehension of a categorical boundary that separates the practice of Cecil Taylor from the practice of Jay-Z. At least, I think I might be reading wrong the important passage in Baraka's "The Changing Same," quoted in part below, that sets the tone and conceptual framework for a music essentialism that would broker the possibility of believing in black popular music as viscerally pleasurable, roots and yet philosophically inadequate for thinking black life beyond the scope of its propertyhood, as opposed or in contradistinction to black art music. It's so simple, yet so troubling, Baraka's formulation of the distinctive expressive actions of black genius, present in the "free" music he adores, absent from "what the cat on the block digs."

> *The implications of content.*
>
> ...But the significant difference is, again, direction, intent, sense of identification ... "kind" of consciousness. And that's what it's about; consciousness. What are you with (the word Con-With/Scio-Know). The "new" musicians are self-conscious. Just as the boppers were. Extremely conscious of self. They are more conscious of a total self (or want to be) than the R&B people who, for the most part, are all-expression. Emotional expression. . . . But at its best and most expressive, the

> New Black Music is expression, and expression of reflection as well. What is presented is a consciously proposed learning experience. ... It is no wonder that many of the new Black musicians are or say they want to be "Spiritual Men" (some of the boppers embraced Islam), or else they are interested in the Wisdom Religion itself, i.e., the rise to spirit. **It is expanding the consciousness of the given that they are interested in, not merely expressing what is already there, or alluded to. They are interested in the *unknown*. The mystical. ... R&B is about emotion, issues purely out of emotion. New Black Music is also about emotion, but from a different place, and, finally, towards a different end. What these musicians feel is a more complete existence. That is, the digging of everything.** What the wisdom religion preaches. (But the actual New Black Music will be a larger expression. It will include the pretension of The New Music, as actuality, as summoner of Black Spirit, the evolved music of the then evolved people.) *[my emphasis]*

This passage (its roving, stabbing, argument moving via a logic of feel and memory, poetic thinking) begins a discussion of the "emotionalism that seeks freedom" in collectively improvised music; *"the freedom to exist in this"* using the "Black Life Force."

Because what is Baraka talking about—"kind of consciousness"? Writing with the painful, highly punctuated exactness that is an example of what I meant when I referred to his prose exertions at the very start of this (long) essay, he defaults to characteristic blindness around the action of digging and the posture of having arrived at a previously undiscovered level of so-called depth. Perhaps this blindness is characteristic of the self-consciously avant-garde, but more important for the purpose of my "argument" is the arresting explicitness of the move to dissociate the expanded consciousness of the New Music from mundane on-the-block varieties of "emotion."

Baraka thus implies the need to isolate certain aspects of the content of black difference from the this-ness of the this within and through which "Ornette, Archie and Cecil" are trying to get free. "Love," in particular, the digging of one thing and the dominant theme of R&B—a gross impediment to the "digging of everything." Let "this missed love that runs through these songs is exactly reflect (sic) of what is the term of love and loving in the Black world of America Twentieth Century"—about love as a syndrome of everyday life lived under the shadow of missed opportunity (to transform or experience transformation/fake transformative forms of intimacy): "how to get through it and to the other side (or maybe not) which for the most part still bees that world"—stand for what the new/different thing opposes with *emotional learning*. For Baraka, the learning is otherworldly insofar as it commences with the recognition that getting through the everyday is a process of reorganizing emotional values so that the fulfillment of individual desires as "freedom," not love, becomes the deepest feeling in our lives. Getting through is not endurance but the capacity to transfuse emotion beyond quotidien barriers (if it is possible to speak of emotion as released from the time-space context where it happens, which this discourse presumes and recommends). Freedom is an emotion that has to do with the desire to achieve a conscious state of living beyond the given relations, given intimacies, given order of social relations, and, crucially, this *freedom is and can only be achieved in conversation and collaboration with other like-minded black people.*

Baraka is so condescending about that which is run-of-the-mill in R&B—boring sex events, partying—and by extension in black life (which is ironic, given his pre-occupation with the practice of collective improvisation) that I guess what is being called for, back of all this kind of music thinking, is a kind of domination by poet legislator. But that's undesirable because it is still domination (and by a class of persons who declare themselves to be fundamentally opposed to governance), impossible because of the general scarcity of poets. I'm saying there is only one "kind of consciousness," like Baraka already knows when he says in the same goddamn essay: "We are moved and directed by our total response to the possibility of all effects." The achievement of the individual breakthrough in thinking beyond the given circumstances and curtailments of everyday life, as "love," is made via encounter with the presence and possibility of transformation of the given (fucked up), unreconstructed or plain. To go out or deep is a reckoning with the regular, a mode of existing that paradoxically enjoys the unreconstructed or plain because it reeks of the place from which it came, the interior reach, which is an edge or outside; before and what will always be. This must be what it means to have blackness as a value.

"There is a history of the embrace of degraded pleasure." What about the ways in which the R&B of my mind, today, is undermined by its own exuberant supplantation by the *vulgar* practice of Jay-Z—right-before-our-eyes capitalization of the value of black love and (of) hustle; he is a hedge fund. His vulgar practice is irrelevant to elaborating the love between us because it does not differentiate between transformative intimacy that is future-oriented and the consumable performance of black presence, which is always oriented toward what is already known about the black, all the symbolic causes of our danger. The vulgar practice is a fire-sale on the "all emotion" of the old R&B, trafficking in what Baraka views as the small-minded romantic hysteria of regular feeling (Beyonce's *Lemonade*) and peppers the old feelings, sweetens the deal, via performance of an emotional and affective repertoire that emerges from the time of rap music, alone. A terse awareness of the market value of the violence and isolation that gives our love its peculiarity. "The slave is the object to whom anything can be done, whose life can be squandered with impunity": the slave is "property of enjoyment." "I know that we the new slaves." So, for all our willingness to admit the occult status of James Brown or Prince or Michael Jackson or Marvin Gaye, all in a disputed relation to the status of Billie Holiday, Nina Simone, Aretha Franklin, we do not know what to do about Beyoncé/Jay-Z/Kanye. Beyoncé/Jay-Z/Kanye declines to spend one's life reflecting on the truth of one's historical objecthood. Beyoncé/Jay-Z/Kanye heralds disrespect for/displacement of bluesy endurance and love of freedom, which implies consent to defer freedom's arrival. Any variant of a rich nigga type ethics refuses this infinite deferral.

Rap music is included in what we are talking about when we talk about the Music in its "ontic" variation/s; we must talk about it as a black social and spiritual haven—it is given as haven or refuge, though it may make no explicit claim for itself about its sociopolitical relevance outside the generic claim "we.made.it." If we believe that black social life is black thought as Fred Moten asserts in "Blackness and Poetry," then rap being made today is evidence of unification of ontic and characteristically crass and troubled aspects of the contemporary thought project of blackness, such that it remains strikingly, if accidentally, true that *the song and the people is the same*. I'm saying, or rather, asking, isn't it possible that the complex knit of song and people, today, confesses a contraction in the imagination of freedom from the status of property, plunging headlong into the terrifying convergence of blackness with capital the likes of which we have never seen and have not begun to understand? Rap music in the new formation invites motivated consumers—there is no distinction here between artist and consumer, there is no distinction here between the sacred black (male) expurgation of the inauthentic R&B-type lame forms of emotion and the invitation to simulate/sample/make copies of the raw or real or "true" experience of the black, or, black life, such as Murda Beatz, such as *FL Studio is a machine object whose sole function is simulation of organic feeling, it has no blackness, or, what is the stuff of life of a trap beat*—to participate in ritual conflation of "enjoyment" with disgust.

I'm asking whether the music we have, today, not the music we used to have or the music we imagine, continues to offer up, as it actually is, something we might look to as a prophecy of being different in blackness, some impossible writing on the air like thought balloons. It is my hope that thinking moves over and past this iteration of our music like a tongue, its serious and interior disturbance, its delicious threat, in order to sense the future. For this to happen, we must agree to think about the work we have asked the Music to do, whether it is still able to do that work, and how that work might be done elsewhere.

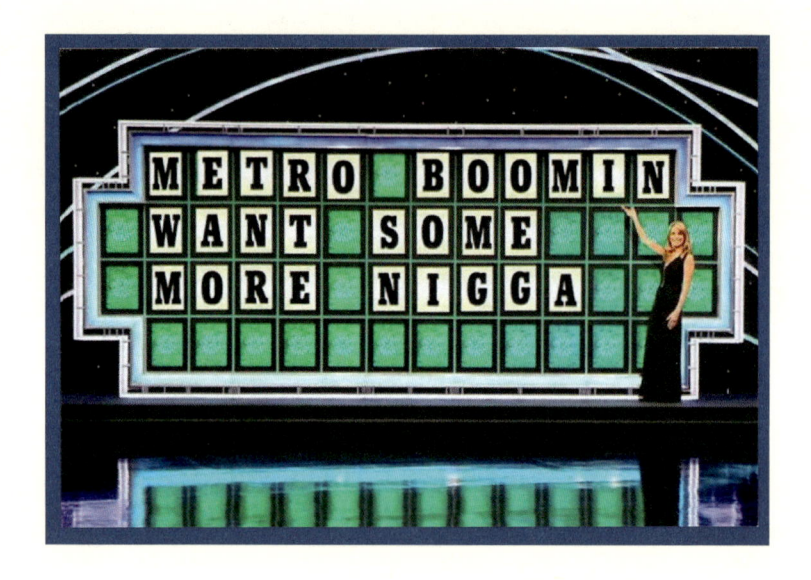

The statement of this objection leads me to say that I think this difficulty, wherever it is felt, to be entitled to the greatest weight. It is alone a sufficient objection to the ordinance. It is my own objection. This mode of commemorating Christ is not suitable to me. That is reason enough why I should abandon it.

— Ralph Waldo Emerson

Most of what I have to say and think about very recent rap music, trap music in particular, is infused/fused with the thinking of Jace Clayton. I will not attempt to distinguish the exact points of our agreement and disagreement. OUR collaborative thinking and friendship, which initially took the form of a challenging and generative correspondence,* transformed vague uneasiness, aversion, disgust with the continuing power of the Music to determine or settle thought about how black persons who wish to change their minds—thus to de-subjectify as Judith Butler puts it—might do so through the practices discovered and demonstrated in black art, into an explosive formal search for new ways to express my thinking about emotional commitment and response to rap music. More than that, I began to look for new ways to represent the connection between sounds and words, watching/listening to (other) black people speak, speaking (to other black people), loving a person who is black, investment in the survival of black persons, belief in magic. Cosmic sparks that abstractly cause objects to affect one another are the energy of new thinking (this inconceivable action is absolute reality). We must have access to that spark to burn up old thinking. Jace is the messenger, but the message cannot be got from the commands of the messenger, who is only an expression of the receptive possibilities of the one who receives the message.

----

* Which began: "'Blue Suede' is perfect in its understanding and, therefore, of very limited use—I'm saying, if what you're interested in is something like freedom. And I'm not saying this about the lyrics. I'm saying what is black music for?"

I quit, now, capitulation to the legend of the Music as a superior space for investigating, as digging, knowledge of freedom. Let the work of sociological description and literary critical "reading" continue elsewhere, and far be it from me. Professional habits of criticism and thought cannot account at all for elements of black music that *have no form* that hasn't already been constitutive of black legibility. What if we were to say, *This sound is unrecognizable to me; I don't know what this black sound is; I don't know what it wants; I don't know whether it is saying what it says it is saying.* What if I gave it that much respect?

I quit the pretense of belief in the divisibility of black consciousness along the lines of high and low that accompanies orthodox black music thinking as a ruse of purity. I renounce that division and embrace the hollow affect of the R&B of my mind, the R&B I never liked, a hollow that I think, now, was the starting place of a bend or fold that would lead toward thinking the abrasive lure of black music in its whole brokenness, the abrasion that must be the beginning of thinking, whenever it begins.

Instead, I begin from Ahmir (Questlove) Thompson's statement: "hip hop has taken over black music."* There is nothing happening

---

* He makes this claim in part one of a four-part essay featured on *Vulture* over four weeks. In the other parts Thompson claims that: *a)* "hip-hop mainly rearranges symbolic freight on the black starliner." Take this phrase to mean in all its possible multiplicity: hip hop does not create new symbolic information, plays no new language games; hip hop recycles images of the black past and moves them around on its own discursive field in some of the ways I try to describe in this essay; alternatively, hip hop is a sham revolutionary enterprise, a cuckoo mix of entrepreneurship and fantastical domination role-play in which masses of black people buy into a doomed transportation scheme; *b)* black cool has ceased to be a locus of innovative tension in American racial discourse; *c)* "Hip-hop, after beginning as a site of resistance, has become, in some sense, the new disco. The signifiers are different, of course. Hip-hop has come to know itself largely via certain notions of capitalist aspiration, braggadocio, and

in contemporary black popular music that doesn't have something to do with rap formally, technologically, or stylistically. Not only is rap fully integrated into the segregationist music industrial categories of "soul" and "R&B," it dominates those categories: its global and national popularity control the output and availability of all forms of black popular music. It is hard to hear (in the senses of both find and understand as black) black music that does not sound like rap music. Black music that is formally distinct from rap, such as the experimental music of Matana Roberts, sounds somewhat ineffectively into rap's vortical socio-symbolic domination of the black music space. What is the performative relation of Roberts' project, which takes a jazz-based approach to be fruitful for historical investigation of blackness as quest for freedom (how did the black inside come to pass?), to trap music's disinterest in the whole notion of cause and effect (don't matter/don't care how this happened/*nothing could shift this slide into oblivion*) in favor of a vicious yet flip insistence on the intractability of black misery (yah yah yah yah yah/push me to the edge, all my friends are dead/look at me, fuck on me)? I find myself wanting the experimental music people to answer for this, although twenty years ago they would not have had to. Rap music is, therefore, in a contemporary-specific, hegemonic formal and mimetic position: you can't shake it off. It is exceedingly difficult to credibly develop a node of black expression that does not articulate a relation to it. Or, alternatively, we are forced to think into the silence about it when an artist is silent about it, which can be a cause for celebration but does not deny rap's power in absence.

---

macho posturing, which are different notes than those struck in disco. But the aesthetic ruthlessness, the streamlining of concept, is similar. What began as a music animated mainly by a spirit of innovation now has factory specifications. Hip-hop, more product than process, means something increasingly predictable, which means that it means less and less."

JAZZ IS DEAD and the related assertion that (t)rap music is alive and giving us the equivalent of this:

In the beautiful writhe of the black spirit-energy sound the whole cellar was possessed and animated. Things flew through the air.

My students tell me that XXXTentacion is not a rapper. They say he "just does this thing in the house" and "puts it on the internet." (Someone else says, "Travis Scott is a rapper," and I am baffled: Travis Scott *sings*... Another thing that has happened—merger of rhetorical positions, merger of the singing position of the lover with the speaking position of the polemicist.) My students understand something about the coming situation, this nothing, as Giorgio Agamben works the question of the now through his reading of Paul, that I am not equipped to understand.

What is happening is partly machine. A rapper is part machine, part apparatus; he is not exactly nothing but a man. My students are twenty. When I am in the room with these twenty-year-old women who listen only to rap music (like me, now, taken in by it in a way that I was not when I was twenty, now that it appears to me as a code or key, a fully developed language of life, a zone of information conveyed or delivered through the body by overtaxed or exhausted masters of the machine: Metro Boomin, Sonny Digital, Mike Will-Made-It, 808 Mafia, Boi-1da). The trap music producer exhales a pervasive—diffuse and dilute—sonic/affective atmosphere through the machines. Trap beat-making is a methodology of surround; so that we find ourselves in a club that we have not chosen to enter, though we have paid. The club is everywhere and everyone is in it. It is put on the internet; it flies through the air.

A cursory scroll through the discography of the producer Lex Luger bears out the extraordinary historical speed at which the trap surround has developed and spread, the numerosity and thickness that belong to its presence. A sub-bass drone accompanies words the rapper says (deftness, sleight of hand with the limited discursive materials of consumable black life, more about which below), borrowed from the beat-making repertoire of electronic dance music, which thrives on investment in the pushy invasion that occurs when sine waves deployed in vast open spaces make contact with bodies that intend to absorb thump, bodies invested in turning toward the direction of the sound, catching the wave of bass between them as intimacy/sex/euphoria. To make much or everything of a single ambient tone, to throw it about a cavernous space. Various studies in contrast/noise and synth overtake or emphasize the fundamentality of the drop. In rap music, the open space of the club is the world space of the music industry, the anti-club, *everywhere*. In trap music, bass is threatened by the interference/meddling of the machine. Trap music's busyness or tchchiness, the way in which it ticks.

I am talking about now and about the future, about the beautiful and terrible "kind of consciousness" this new black music surfaces.

Speaking of "musical togetherness" then—even and especially as it is presently trafficked by a constellation of super rappers and producers who are indisputably mighty rock stars—think about Drake and Future's "Diamonds Dancing." Think of Future's extraordinary prolificity for which trapping is example and symbolical foundation. Think black people who are "rock stars" think Hendrix chart domination supergroup, then think *producer tag*: Metro Boomin Want Some More Nigga. Think *homo economicus*. Think Jay-Z and Kanye West's *Watch the Throne* as evidence of the possibility of a Drake and Future tour (think about the roots of all these words); think a realm where there are no women who are not strippers and drug mules and things like bikes one man swaps with another man. Future's "Covered N Money," "Blasé," "I Serve the Base," "Digital

Dash" (its bassline recalls R&B troubles, ironically synchronized with the characteristic fast-twinkling hi-hat synth that defines trap beats, propels the sensation of perpetual procurement), "Supertrapper." Think the ethereal contemporary presence of the words "black death" and "black lives."

> nags in the back of my mind when i'm reading black nihilism on the train at 9am—this is the sound of no hope no futurity. black life as black death, drained of pleasure & presence—sexual/sensual intimacies get violently muted/displaced into lean and everybody's like of Future, the vibes, the feels, as if our appreciation of him hinges upon that sensual sonic aspect and not the fucked up sad awfulness of it all.

What if this music, Future's *DS2*, the Drake/Future *What a Time to Be Alive*, Vince Staples' *Summertime '06*, Kanye West's *Life of Pablo*, the numerous individual points that are sounds and words that emerge from laptops, artists who live within this surround, the formation that is trap music—more, there are more coming—speak the dimension, let us displace Heidegger and call it a metaphysical zone of intent, let's call it "possibility"—let's call it *now*, cracked time of where we are and where we are going now. We don't have the words for how broken. And yet we are warned.

In "Diamonds Dancing" the main action takes place in the spine: a study of the male torso, draped in rocks. Think what weight sounds like, think what synth is, think sirens and explosions and gunclap and distortion, the wormy clicking snares we cannot perceive as time-keeping sounds because the time they keep is machine time, think the pressurized squeeze of optimally lean dancer's muscle/twitch, or movement around the world of the culture of drugs and guns that becomes the performative condition upon which all representation of human activity must take place. Think, *what it would mean to allow this formation to contour my understanding of what freedom is and thus what thinking is, allowing that—not if, that—it constitutes thinking, gesture act and art.* Think, this is the formation that is the air of now feeling which we have no choice but to breathe as life and thus to celebrate, but what does it mean to be in and not of it, to love and refuse it: *to be in and out at the same time?*

> the beat only kicks in briefly ([and] is shuddering + emphatic when it does), and the song recedes slow over that squirmy synth towards the end. the tide is way out. we see dead fish in the sand.

Shuddering. "Diamonds Dancing" is a song-space no one could stand up in; shuddering, or/and a tiny burst of air pushed out of the throat, not a sigh, a breathy grunt (uh or eh or uch yuh or yea or yay, think sublinguistic expressions of affirmation or continuity). A song that, slow to begin, *never really moves*, a song without momentum (without moment?) where human vocal presence is initiated by a typical pronouncement of profound boredom that accompanies achievement of full sexual and economic potency (I'm at a stage of my life where I feel like I can conquer anything and everything / sippin on Dom Perignon for no reason / poppin tags upper echelon for no reason). Inside this middle of the club blank space, a falling down or staggering sound space without proper structure, Drake does something verbally surprising. He takes up (for rehearsal) a cranky and specific soul/R&B narrative of romantic devastation and discord: *You know what I need from you when I get home. And yet you will not give it.* Then the song space gathers again, the beat drops as a head-scratching instant of dance music entering a tiny crack in the space of Future's developing story about his inability to feel (I got so many bad bitches that I barely want em / I'm barely paying attention baby on this substance / I know you spent some time putting on your makeup and your outfit). At three minutes, when the song should properly begin to end, Drake mutters or whispers into a minute-30 second recession (nearly half a song-length), a counterpoint, and also a coda, to Future's anhedonia—a neurotic and highly specific complaint. It is "all emotion": an encrypted, limited character invention of rich insult. I love to hear black couples fight.

DEATH * DROP * PAIN

"TO DROP": lose control over digital manipulation of; lose control over the musculature of one's body/to fall down or faint/to lose consciousness; to render another person unconscious, as to knock upside the head; to kill ("there were five persons taken in one house; the father the mother and the suckling child they knocked on head"). You *drop* and so it hurts to hear every time

bitches aint shit but hoes / I been known this ...

... finna kill a nigga / walkin to his mom's tonight ...

...death row til they put you in the Pikachu to fry...

...coulda been a felon / sellin nickles offa Linden / nigga fuck that...

all I wanted was them Jordans with the Blue Suede on em (RPT)

Listening obsessively to Vince Staples' "Blue Suede" and the music of Vince Staples more generally caused me to struggle to materialize my thoughts about rap as a force that propels my own thinking away from music as a way OUT. Listening to "Blue Suede" made me think, this music is fucked up, it's not about freedom at all, it's not collaboratively representing the concept of initiating freedom by making something out of nothing and listening and thought (this is how Mackey sees jazz, I think, this is why we cling to it, as beautiful evidence of invention), it's not a general example of how freedom might be achieved. This person's cry is profoundly isolated, speaks to an emotional situation that is desire, which, Anne Carson says, is about what we are never going to have; about what never comes.

Thinking and feeling in an emergency listening to "Blue Suede" (I had a little nursing baby, my marriage was crumbling), it spoke to me from a place of pure feeling, raw nerves; it spoke to me in that place. This teenaged rapper from California (!) caused something new to begin in me; the sounds he made sounded like life, sounded like now. I was at a loss for words to say what this song was and was not to me and for me. How to say this tripped out singularity blows my mind, but I do not rely on it. How to say what I learn from this is caution; I can take no strategy from this, poetic or otherwise for thinking a better social life as an artist or human being. And this twist, the energetic fright Vince gives, is exhilarating.

At this point it's useful to invoke Emily Dickinson.

> There is a pain—so utter—
> It swallows substance up—
> Then covers the Abyss with Trance—
> So Memory can step
> Around—across—opon it—
> As One within a Swoon—
> Goes safely—where an open eye—
> Would drop Him—Bone by Bone—

Dickinson works in an emotional shorthand, she develops her own affects and "cadence" around a relatively slim repertoire of words, number of words. She reforms, represses, reorganizes the meaning of those words by moving stresses around, deforming the ballad form, performing a kind of lyric screaming. She composes on a field upon which she is the only player in broad strokes, made over top the primary practice of what is called poetry and outside its game. Dickinson is, therefore, an example of a privacy and singularity that is entirely foreclosed by the invocation of the "blackness" of any art practice. In rap music there is no inner space, no privacy, no singularity; there is, far in the future, the destruction of these conditions; there is the future. For us, Dickinson's an example of nothing. Yet we hear her ripping sound in our mind's eye as a harbinger of what could happen, yet.

If what is called "flow" is the shared ground between Dickinson and Staples, the mechanism of flow should obviously be brought out (explained?) to explain the connection and de-fuse the explosive hierarchical possibilities that inhere in setting Emily up against Vince. This is not obvious to me. In a perfect song, lyric and sound lock together as flow so that the sensuous element, the mode of delivering the pleasure of the song, the way it enters the body and can be enjoyed, can't be separated from lyrics which ostensibly "describe" the rapper's "life" or "feelings" or "thoughts." "All I wanted was them Jordans with the Blue Suede on em." This is so easy to hear. Jordans, the adolescent wish for special ones, blue suede ones, Elvis, love and theft. "Flow" is something we have to get rid of in the effort to make sense of how love can be found in and through this music.

A song like "Blue Suede" attempts to work in Dickinsonian ways; it cannot, although it SOUNDS like it does. Vince's dexterity, his flow, his dark dark humor, the stuttering/scratchy grind that attempts to perforate the wail that swallows up loudness (producer=Marvin "Hagler" Thomas); these language and sonic acts work in the register of command. But achieving the "commanding certificate" (as Emerson says) is a cheap rap music trick that attempts to circumvent the grammars of race and structural poverty. (Ain't nobody triller than Metro / ain't nobody triller than Scooter; If Young Metro don't trust you / Ima shoot you.) There's an emotional and ideological grid that

Vince Staples has access to, but hasn't built. That grid is structured by the axes of being / living as black and the practice of representing blackness. Vince hasn't built it—and it's not his fault—yet he plays or practices a black game which is also the game of *repeating what we already know, repeating facts to which it is possible to nod our heads, facts such as "the music and the people is the same."* We watch him work a terrifying manipulation of ideological and emotional materials that are fundamentally out of his control and so drop him, Emily says, BONE by BONE. That is what it is to look, if you look, into the abyss, the organized inside space of blackness.

Which is whatever you want it to be; it is a "trap" in the same sense that trap music proposes as authentic black life the deadly workaday circuit of street-level drug dealing to pay the bills and, with luck, hard work and a ride-or-die trap queen, bootstrap up to the (clownish) status of rich nigga.

Future's "I Serve the Base" from 2015's *DS2*:

> They should've told you I was just a trap nigga
> I'm in the White House shootin' craps niggas
> I gave up on my conscience gotta live with it
> [...]
> They should've told you I was on the pill
> They should've told you I was on the Lear
> I serve cocaine in some Reeboks
> I'm full of so much chronic, need a detox
> I serve the base, I serve the base
> I serve the base, I serve the base

Whatever you want. I serve that, for money, for a nihilistic, endlessly repetitive and narcotized kind of peace. I surround us with the call to recede into the persona of whatever it is one serves.

Juvenile—Respect My Mind, Ha, Back Dat Azz Up (ft. Mannie Fresh, Lil' Wayne), Rich Niggaz, Enemy Turf (w/ Lil Wayne)
Ghostface Killah—Stroke of Death
Rick Ross—Hustlin'
Ace Hood—Hustle Hard
Juicy J (ft. Lil Wayne, 2 Chainz)—Bandz a Make Her Dance
Jay-Z and Kanye West—Ni**as in Paris
Chief Keef—I Don't Like
Kanye West—*Yeezus*, *The Life of Pablo*
A$AP Ferg—Shabba, Dump Dump, Plain Jane
Jay-Z (ft. Rick Ross)—Fuckwithmeyouknowigotit
Birdman (ft. Drake)—Money to Blow
Migos—Versace, Bad and Bougee
Rick Ross (ft. Drake)—Aston Martin Music
Lil Wayne (ft. 2 Chainz)—Rich as Fuck
Meek Mill (ft. Rick Ross)—Ima Boss
Meek Mill—Traumatized
Young Thug—Stoner, Danny Glover, Digits, Harambe
Rae Sremmurd—No Flex Zone, Black Beatle
Chris Brown—When a Rich Nigga Want You
Frank Ocean—Pyramids, Nikes, Ivy
Vince Staples—Blue Suede, *Summertime '06*
Lil B—Murder Rate
Future (ft. The Weeknd)—Low Life
Future—*DS2*
Future & Drake—Diamonds Dancing, Digital Dash
Travis Scott—*Birds in the Trap Sing McKnight*, Butterfly Effect
Desiigner—Panda

SOURCES & ACKNOWLEDGMENTS

SOURCES

Dear Angel of Death is indebted to many texts from which it does not directly quote. Direct quotations from the following texts appear in the essay.

Agamben, Giorgio. *The Time That Remains: A Commentary on the Letter to the Romans.* Trans. Patricia Dailey. Stanford: Stanford University Press, 2005.

Baraka, Amiri. *Black Music.* New York: Morrow, 1968.

---. *Blues People: Negro Music in White America.* 1963. New York: Harper, 1999.

---. *Digging: the Afro-American Soul of American Classical Music.* Berkeley: University of California Press, 2009.

Baucom, Ian. *Specters of the Atlantic: Finance Capital, Slavery and the Philosophy of History.* Durham: Duke University Press, 2005.

Benjamin, Walter. "On the Concept of History." *Walter Benjamin: Selected Writings Volume 4, 1938-1940.* Eds. Howard Eiland and Michael W. Jennings. Cambridge: Belknap-Harvard, 2006. 389-400.

Butler, Judith. *The Psychic Life of Power: Theories in Subjection.* Stanford: Stanford University Press, 1997.

Chandler, Nahum Dimitri. *X-The Problem of the Negro as a Problem for Thought.* New York: Fordham University Press, 2013.

Deleuze, Gilles. *The Fold: Leibniz and the Baroque.* Minneapolis: University of Minnesota Press, 1992.

---. *Foucault.* Trans. Seán Hand. Minneapolis: University of Minnesota Press, 1988.

Dickinson, Emily. *The Poems of Emily Dickinson: Reading Edition.* Ed. R.W. Franklin. Cambridge: Belknap, 2005.

Du Bois, W.E.B. *Black Reconstruction in America, 1860-1880*. 1935. New York: Free Press, 1998.

Emerson, Ralph Waldo. "Nature." *Essays and Lectures*. New York: Library of America, 1983.

---. "The Lord's Supper" (Sermon CLXII). Emerson Central. <https://emersoncentral.com>.

Future. "I Serve the Base." *DS2*. Epic Records, 2015. [pp. 149]

---. "Diamonds Dancing." *What a Time to Be Alive*. Cash Money Records, 2015.

Ghostface Killah. "We Made It." *Supreme Clientele*. Epic Records, 2000.

Gilroy, Paul. *The Black Atlantic: Modernity and Double-Consciousness*. Cambridge: Harvard University Press, 1993.

Hayden, Robert. "Runagate Runagate." *Collected Poems*. Ed. Frederick Glaysher. New York: Liveright, 1985.

Heidegger, Martin. *Poetry, Language, Thought*. Trans. Albert Hofstadter. New York: Harper, 2001.

Heuving, Jeanne. "An Interview with Nathaniel Mackey." *Contemporary Literature* 53:2 (Summer 2012): 207-236.

Howe, Susan. *The Birth-mark: Unsettling the Wilderness in American Literary History*. Middletown: Wesleyan University Press, 1993.

Lil' Uzi Vert. "XO Tour Llif3." *Luv Is Rage 2*. Generation Now and Atlantic Records, 2017.

Mackey, Nathaniel. *Bass Cathedral*. New York: New Directions, 2008.

---. *From a Broken Bottle Traces of Perfume Still Emanate: Volumes 1-3*. New York: New Directions, 2010.

---. *Discrepant Engagement: Dissonance, Cross-Culturality, and Experimental Writing*. Tuscaloosa: University of Alabama Press, 1993.

Mbembe, Achille. *On the Postcolony*. Berkeley, CA: University of California Press, 2001.

Migos. "Bad and Bougee." *Culture*. Quality Control Music, 300 Entertainment, and YRN Tha Label, 2017.

Moten, Fred. "Blackness and Nothingness (Mysticism in the Flesh)." *South Atlantic Quarterly* 112:4 (Fall 2013). 737-780. Duke University Journals.

---. "Blackness and Poetry." *The Holloway Series/Mixed Blood Project*. University of California, Berkeley. <https://www.youtube.com/watch?v=Su7iCumqLvo>.

---. "The Case of Blackness." *Criticism* 50:2 (Spring 2008): 177-218.

---. *In the Break: The Aesthetics of the Black Radical Tradition*. Minneapolis: Minnesota University Press, 2003.

Nancy, Jean-Luc. *Listening*. Trans. Charlotte Mandell. Fordham University Press, 2007.

Nielsen, Aldon Lynn. *Black Chant: Languages of African-American Postmodernism*. Cambridge: Cambridge University Press, 1997.

Ricouer, Paul. Memory, History, Forgetting. Trans. Kathleen Blamey and David Pellauer. Chicago: University of Chicago Press, 2006)

Scott, Travis. "3500." *Rodeo*. Grand Hustle/Epic, 2015.

Sexton, Jared. "The Social Life of Social Death: On Afro-Pessimism and Black Optimism." *InTensions* 5.0 (Fall/Winter 2011): 1-47. AMPD at York University. <yorku.ca/intent/index>.

Staples, Vince. "Blue Suede." *Hell Can Wait*. Def Jam Recordings, 2014.

Steamer, Hank. "How to Dress Well: Loss Leader." *FADER* 81 (August/September 2012).

Thompson, Ahmir. "How Hip-Hop Failed Black America, Parts I-IV." Vulture.com.

Warren, Kenneth. "Does African-American Literature Exist?" *The Chronicle of Higher Education*. <https://www.chronicle.com/article/Does-African-American/126483>.

West, Kanye. *Yeezus*. Def Jam Recordings, 2013.

Wilderson, III, Frank B. and Saidiya Hartman. "The Position of the Unthought." *Qui Parle* 13:2 (Spring/Summer 2003): 183-201.

Williams, Raymond. *Marxism and Literature*. Oxford: Oxford University Press, 1977.

XXXTentacion. "Look at Me!" *Revenge*. Empire Distribution, 2017.

ACKNOWLEDGMENTS

This book is for my son, Isaac Agrippa Freeman Leslie.

There is no fear in love, but perfect love casts out fear. For fear has to do with punishment, and whoever fears has not been perfected in love.

These are the names of people who kept Isaac and me going during the time of this book: Nancy Farma, Stacy Armoogan, Latisa Gilmore, Catherine Pond, Meredith Gray, Eddie Laguna, Patricia Powlette and Deja Ross at The Co-op School, Hannah MacLagger, Dr. Aruby Odom White, Santi White, Trevor Andrew, Naim Ali White, Radek Andrew, Cheryl Jones Walker, Imani Perry, Joy Phillips, Hope Wilson, erica kaufman, Lorrin Thomas, Samantha Corson, Karen Kelly, Litia Perta, Aracelis Girmay, Anna Moschovakis, Laura Henriksen, Stacy Szymaszek, Nicole Wallace, Matt Longabucco, Robin Tremblay-McGaw, Amy Wilson, Stefania Heim, and Kofi Taha. There are many many others.

Those who have guided and aided me include Ammiel Alcalay, Joan Retallack, Fred Moten, Joan Richardson, Eric Lott, Herman Bennett, Claudia Rankine, Eileen Myles, Erica Hunt, Lyn Hejinian, Myung Mi Kim, and Elizabeth Willis. Jerry Gafio Watts (1953-2015) was and is an example to me in thinking, teaching and caring for others; I miss him so much.

Thanks to the editors who previously published work that appears in this book: *Belladonna*, BOMB Magazine, Boston Review, Chicago Review, Harper's Magazine, The Poetry Foundation*, and WFMT Radio Network's PoetryNow podcast, The Racial Imaginary Institute, *The Volta*, and *ythm Journal*.

I am grateful, too, for the support of The Whiting Foundation.

Dollbaby 7

Endings 45

Dear Angel of Death 67

SOURCES & ACKNOWLEDGMENTS 153